THE GREAT LIVES SERIES

Great Lives biographies shed an exciting new light on the many dynamic men and women whose actions, visions, and dedication to an ideal have influenced the course of history. Their ambitions, dreams, successes, and failures, the controversies they faced and the obstacles they overcame are the true stories behind these distinguished world leaders, explorers, and great Americans.

Other biographies in the Great Lives Series

CHRISTOPHER COLUMBUS: The Intrepid Mariner

JOHN F. KENNEDY: Courage in Crisis

SALLY RIDE: Shooting for the Stars

HARRIET TUBMAN: Call to Freedom

MIKHAIL GORBACHEV: The Soviet Innovator

A special thanks to educators Dr. Frank Moretti, Ph.D., Associate Headmaster of the Dalton School in New York City; Dr. Paul Mattingly, Ph.D., Professor of History at New York University; and Barbara Smith, M.S., Assistant Superintendent of the Los Angeles Unified School District for their contributions to the Great Lives series.

ABRAHAM LINCOLN
THE FREEDOM PRESIDENT

Susan Sloate

FAWCETT COLUMBINE
NEW YORK

For middle school readers

A Fawcett Columbine Book
Published by Ballantine Books

Library of Congress Catalogue Card Number: 89-90822

ISBN: 0-449-90375-3

Cover design and illustration by Paul Davis

Manufactured in the United States of America

First Edition: September 1989

10 9 8 7 6 5 4 3 2

TABLE OF CONTENTS

Abraham Lincoln was the first president to be assassinated, the first president born in Kentucky, the first and only president to have a patent, the first president to have a beard, and the first Republican president. This photograph by Matthew Brady was used for the engraving of Lincoln's head on the five-dollar note

1

A Murder Plot in Baltimore

LIKE MANY MURDER plots, this one began with a whisper and a boast.

The whisper of discontent came from many Southerners who were enraged at the results of the 1860 presidential election. Abraham Lincoln, a Republican and a Northerner, had been elected president of the United States. Though Lincoln's anti-slavery platform had helped him narrowly win the election by carrying the vote in the Northern states, his popularity was sharply limited. As news of Lincoln's success spread through the country, pro-slavery Southerners angrily cried that his election as the sixteenth president of the United States would mean civil war! The states of the South would never accept Abraham Lincoln, an abolitionist, as their president!

The boast of a plot to assassinate President Lincoln came from the lips of a man named Sipriano Fernandino. He was the house barber at Barnum's Hotel in Baltimore, Maryland. Like many Southerners, he had been increasingly angered by pressure from North-

1

erners to free the Southern black slaves and to prevent the spread of slavery into western territories which would soon become states. Fernandino believed the entire economic system of the South would collapse if it were forced to give up slave labor. Wealthy plantation owners counted on black slaves to work in their large cotton, rice, and tobacco fields, and they feared the cost of non-slave labor would destroy their profits.

Many Southerners believed that the eleven states which made up the South, and later the Confederacy, would have to secede from or leave the Union, and form a separate country in order to continue slavery. If the South were to secede, the United States would then consist of the eighteen remaining free Northern states which did not allow slavery.

Heated debates erupted in barrooms and parlors about the best way to preserve the South's traditional way of life. There was an intense rivalry between the industrial North and the agricultural South. Some Southerners quietly agreed that killing President-elect Lincoln before he took office was the solution to maintaining slavery in the South.

Fernandino spoke to many such troublemakers in the weeks following Lincoln's election. Eventually Fernandino met with a wealthy, aristocratic older man who represented a number of other people like himself. These men seriously believed that a Lincoln presidency would spell disaster for the Southern way of life, and they wanted to prevent Lincoln from taking office in March 1861.

Fernandino boasted that he was just the man to solve the South's problems of the newly elected president. The barber assured the wealthy man that the South would not have to take such a drastic step as seceding from the Union. With a handpicked band of men, Fernandino said he could destroy Maryland's railroads and kill President Lincoln, too. Then Washington, the nation's capital, would be in Southern hands and the North, without a leader, would be crippled. There would be no need for further bloodshed, and the South would be free to continue as it always had.

The wealthy man and his friends felt that Fernandino's boast made sense. They wanted to avoid bloodshed as much as possible, but they also wanted to stop a president who would free the slaves and thereby devastate the South's economy. The men offered Fernandino their financial support, but insisted on remaining in the background. Fernandino, delighted with a job that he felt would make him a hero, began to recruit men for the sinister murder plot. Fortunately for President-elect Abraham Lincoln, the barber was careless in his recruiting.

Though Fernandino was careful to tell potential co-conspirators only that they would help to destroy the Maryland railroads, word of the planned murder began to leak out. A railroad worker with Northern sympathies heard of the plot and reported it to his superiors. These men in turn reported their knowledge of the plot to a railroad detective named Allan Pinkerton, a Scotsman who guarded trains for the Philadelphia, Wilmington, and Baltimore Railroad.

When Detective Pinkerton heard about the plot to attack the railroads and kill Lincoln, he immediately dispatched several of his best agents to Baltimore, Maryland to find out more about Fernandino's plan. Pinkerton's men, working under assumed names, pretended great sympathy for the South as they chatted with other customers at the bar in Barnum's Hotel. The secret agents declared that they were ready to defend the South to the death.

One agent named Harry Davies, using an alias, soon found himself in the center of a group of pro-slavery Baltimore men who had an intense hatred for Lincoln. Would he be interested in joining them in a special mission to destroy three Maryland railroads?

Davies agreed heartily, hoping the Baltimore men would reveal more of the plot to him. They did. Davies soon found himself at a special meeting of the conspirators led by Fernandino. In addition to destroying the railroads, they would put an end to the unwelcome Northern influence by killing Abraham Lincoln. Their assassination plot revolved around the route of the train bringing Lincoln and his family from their home in Springfield, Illinois to Washington for his inauguration. Fernandino had read in the newspapers that Lincoln planned to speak from the rear of his train when it pulled into Baltimore.

After explaining the plan to the conspirators, Fernandino solemnly passed around a hat with eight markers inside, seven white and one red. Each man was to take a marker and then keep his choice secret. The one who held the red marker knew his assignment—to shoot President-elect Lincoln as he spoke from the rear platform of the train.

Fernandino had not told his men the exact truth. The hat contained three red markers, not one. That way, if one assassin backed out of the plot, there were two others ready to murder the president. He was taking no chances that Lincoln would reach Washington alive.

Agent Davies tensed as the hat reached him. He took a deep breath as he dipped his hand inside. He wanted no part in the killing of Lincoln, none at all. Slowly he opened his fist. The marker was white. He breathed a sigh of relief.

In the meantime, Detective Pinkerton had set up headquarters in Baltimore and coordinated a gigantic effort as his agents reported their information to him. He ordered railroad crews under his agents' supervision to whitewash the railroad bridges. If the conspirators tried to burn the bridges, the whitewash would prevent fire. Pinkerton then sent urgent messages to the presidential train, already en route to Washington. Under no circumstances must Lincoln pass through Baltimore on that train! However, he was to get off the train at Harrisburg, Pennsylvania and give a speech to his supporters as originally planned.

In Harrisburg, on February 21, 1861, men and women gathered quietly in the large, chilly room to hear Lincoln speak. Their voices hushed as an introduction was spoken. They strained forward as a tall, lean man stepped to the podium. For many, it was their first glimpse of Abraham Lincoln, the prairie lawyer from Illinois who had been elected president of the United States nearly three months before.

Abraham Lincoln had just turned fifty-two, stood over six feet tall, and weighed 180 pounds. The straggling dark beard covering his chin was new, suggested in a letter by a little girl who had thought it would add dignity to his face. Lincoln's gray, brooding eyes carried a hint of sadness. His dark hair, only slightly threaded with gray, was coarse. Despite his new position as the nation's most powerful man, the president-elect wore simple clothes.

From the podium, Lincoln peered tensely at the expectant faces. Although his audience was unaware of his inner feelings, the president-elect was irritated. Originally he was scheduled to deliver a speech and then chat afterward with the audience. Now there was to be a change in plans. Lincoln spoke the text of his speech. It was laced with the homespun humor for which he had become famous, and sparkled with the well-turned phrases of an educated man.

The eager listeners who longed for a few moments of conversation with Lincoln were sorely disappointed at the speech's end. Lincoln thanked the audience and then claimed he had a blinding headache. Excusing himself abruptly, he hurried out.

The special train that had brought Lincoln and his family from Springfield was scheduled to continue on to Washington, where he would prepare for his inauguration. The disappointed Harrisburg audience believed that Lincoln had gone to rejoin his family on that train. Instead, Lincoln was driven in a horse-drawn cart to Philadelphia, where he secretly boarded a different train bound for Washington. Pinkerton was to be one of Lincoln's bodyguard on the last and critical stage of the journey.

As Lincoln was hurrying to Philadelphia, Pinkerton was busy with his own tasks. He ordered the telegraph wires cut from Harrisburg to Baltimore. That way, the would-be assassins in Baltimore could have no information about Lincoln's sudden change of plans.

Pinkerton joined the Washington-bound train exactly as planned. He stood alone on the rear platform of the observation car, watching for signals from his agents. As the train neared each crossing and bridge, an agent standing in the darkness flashed a lantern to signal to Pinkerton that all was well. Inside, secluded in a private car, Lincoln worked over his inauguration speech, tucked carefully into a leather gripsack, or bag, that he carried himself.

On the morning of February 23, 1861, Washington was raw and damp, its sidewalks little more than lanes of frozen mud, its inhabitants — black and white — chilled to the bone as they went about their business in the early-morning light.

Elihu B. Washburne, congressman from Illinois, was as chilled as any of them. Stiffening in the dawn cold, he waited impatiently at Washington's train depot and bitterly cursed William Seward, the senator from New York. Seward had promised he would accompany Washburne to meet this all-important train, and then at the last minute, had failed to appear. Washburne's teeth chattered, and his proud beard did little to shield his slowly freezing face.

As the train pulled in, Washburne straightened to his full height. He watched the passengers bustling away and chattering. Not one gave him more than an absentminded glance. Washburne had begun to wonder whether his instructions were correct — was this the train he was supposed to meet? As the ranks of passengers thinned out, he noticed an odd trio approaching him. Instinctively he backed away.

The three men radiated an air of reckless danger. The small man on the left had his hand stuck in the pocket of his thick wool overcoat — an overcoat not thick enough to disguise the outlines of a small pistol hidden underneath. The man on the right was tall and heavyset, and both his hands plunged into the pockets of his coat. Washburne wondered wildly whether this man carried two pistols.

The lanky man in the center of the trio wore a slouch hat tilted over his eyes to hide his face, an effect heightened by his turned-up collar and dark beard. His long, bony fingers tightened on a leather gripsack. Washburne squinted at the man who now looked strangely familiar. Then Washburne's freezing face suddenly relaxed into a warm smile. Abraham Lincoln, the next president of the United States, had safely arrived in Washington.

Lincoln was not happy about the manner of his secret arrival in the nation's capital. Though Pinkerton, the small man, and Ward Hill Lamon, his bodyguard with two guns, were plainly relieved that they had escaped Fernandino's attempted assassination in Baltimore, Lincoln regarded the affair as ridiculous.

The new president understood his lack of popularity in the South. Since election day, newspaper headlines screamed their disapproval, and stacks of hateful letters and death threats filled up Lincoln's law office in Springfield, Illinois.

Yet Lincoln was curiously unconcerned about his own personal safety. When he was first informed of the possible assassination plot brewing in Baltimore, he refused to change his plans. He had chosen to ride a special train from which he could give speeches while on his way to Washington, and that is what he intended to do. It was only when Detective Pinkerton pointed out that Lincoln's wife and children could well be endangered that the president-elect yielded and agreed to sneak into the nation's capital on a different train. This time, like so many other times, Lincoln realized that this was the right thing to do.

Throughout his life, Abraham Lincoln would demonstrate again and again that he did what he thought was right even under the most difficult circumstances. Despite the terrible pressures to sacrifice principle for popularity, Lincoln boldly spoke for the ideals he believed in.

Abraham Lincoln was committed to abolishing the Southern institution of slavery. He firmly believed that all the American states — the Union — should remain united in order to preserve their strength against foreign nations. Though he wanted desperately to avoid a bloody civil war that would wrench the country apart, when it came, he resolved that the greatest issue was preserving the Union. He was determined that the United States of America would remain one country, no matter what the price or how great the heartbreak, because it was the just and correct thing to do.

2

Boy in the Wilderness

THE SOUTH FORK of Nolin Creek was a lonely area in Kentucky, where settlers tried to farm land in an untamed wilderness. It was there, in a tiny, one-room log cabin on Sinking Spring Farm, that Abraham Lincoln was born on February 12, 1809. From his birth, neighbors remarked on the baby's huge dark eyes, inherited from his mother, the former Nancy Hanks.

Nancy took care of the cooking and cleaning the large room that was bedroom, kitchen, dining room, and living room to the Lincolns. The floor was hard-packed dirt. The rough window spaces cut out of the tightly packed logs were covered with cloth. Yet most women did not expect anything more from the Kentucky wilderness, and Nancy was satisfied with her life. While she bent over a large, steaming kettle in a corner of the cabin or washed her family's clothes over a heavy tub, her husband Thomas scratched out a living farming the land they owned. This had been their pattern since they married in 1806.

The Lincolns' first child, Sarah, was born in 1807. Two years later Nancy gave birth to Abraham, named for his grandfather, who was killed by Indians. Some time later Nancy gave birth to a second son who died in infancy. Thomas dug a grave for him that was visible from the Lincoln cabin.

Nancy trusted the teachings of her religion for answers to many of life's cruel turns and told her children that such sorrows were God's will, as her Baptist faith taught. Nancy couldn't read, and she signed legal papers with an X because she couldn't write, either, but she could recite many passages and prayers from the Bible for her children.

Young Abraham thought his mother's belief in the mysterious workings of God made sense. One of his earliest memories was of his terror on the day he went swimming in the creek. He was not strong enough to swim in the deep water, and no one had taught him how to float to the bank of the creek. An older neighbor boy, seeing the frightened lad splashing helplessly in the water, waded in to lift him out. Nancy told Abraham later that his rescue was meant to be, that Providence, or the predetermined design of God, had important tasks in store for him.

Abraham accepted this explanation without question. Though Lincoln followed no particular religious denomination, all his life he would believe in Providence. The belief was so strong that during his presidency he shrugged off most efforts to protect him from assassins. If God meant him to die, then it would happen.

Abraham's father, Thomas, was busy, not only with his farming chores, but with the community duties that he felt were necessary. In addition to the time he spent in discussion with his neighbors, he occupied himself in accumulating land, sitting on juries, and serving on the county slave patrol, which hunted down runaway black slaves and returned them to their white owners. Thus, it was in childhood that young Abraham began to learn about white men owning black men.

Young Abraham began to help his father in the farm duties. One of his first memories was watching his father hoe a field that was once the creek bottom. Abraham's job was to walk behind him and drop pumpkin seeds between the rows of corn. One unfortunate Sunday, a flash flood flowed into the county, washing away both the seeds and the corn. Abraham always remembered this as another illustration of Providence and the hopeless task of man against the working of fate.

Abraham's happiest childhood moments were the two brief periods in 1815 and 1816 when he and his sister were excused from the winter farm chores. Instead, they hiked four miles to the little log schoolhouse on the Cumberland Road. There Abraham learned, slowly and painstakingly, to recite his ABCs under the attention of teacher Zachariah Riney, a fifty-two-year-old slave owner.

Abraham immediately became fascinated with the written word. As he grew up, despite his sketchy schooling, he read whatever he could find, always trying to learn more. Abraham loved to learn, but his constant efforts to improve himself eventually became something that separated him from his father.

One quality that father and son had in common, however, was their delight in storytelling. Thomas Lincoln spent many evenings around a potbellied stove in the community's general store. With the other men gathered around him, he would tell stories, frontier yarns, or homespun jokes. Thomas had a talent for drawing his listeners into the story and describing scenes of great excitement. As soon as he could talk, little Abraham began to imitate his father and memorize the many wonderful tales he heard. Wit and storytelling charm would serve Abraham Lincoln well throughout his life.

Thomas Lincoln's most outstanding quality, however, was his desire to travel and find new places to farm. Like his son, he was always trying to improve his situation in life, but his idea of improvement was finding better land, more land, cheaper land, on which to grow his crops.

However, the Lincolns were forced to moved from their Kentucky home because of a dispute over property rights. Apparently Thomas did not really own the sandy land he and his son farmed. The men who claimed to be the rightful owners were threatening lawsuits. In addition, slavery was spreading through Kentucky, and Thomas feared the competition of farmers who could afford to buy black laborers.

In December of 1816 Thomas packed his family and their possessions into a wagon and led them across the Ohio River to his new claim in the Indiana community of Little Pigeon Creek. The land was more isolated than Kentucky, and the thick forests were full of bears, wild turkeys, and other animals. Thomas hastily set up a three-sided log shelter. A fire burned day and night on the fourth side of the primitive dwelling to keep the family warm at night while Thomas and Abraham worked busily by day constructing a new log cabin as a permanent home.

Though Abraham was only eight years old, he was big enough to swing an ax which he carried with him constantly. Lincoln would later say that his ax was "the most useful instrument." Two months later, the cabin was completed, and the family, with great relief, moved their little household indoors, protected from the bitter Indiana cold.

The year was 1817, and Abraham was growing into a tall spider of a boy who was assuming a greater role in the support of the family. As part of this duty, he armed himself with a shotgun to shoot the wild turkeys that roamed freely across the land. One day in the early spring, he seized his chance to make his first kill. As a turkey strutted toward him in the sunlight, he aimed carefully and pulled the trigger.

The roar filled his ears, and when he lowered the gun he saw the dead bird lying at his feet. Abraham felt sick and realized how ashamed he was for having killed a living creature. He loved birds and animals, often wandered about with them and watched them play, and did not like the idea of killing them — even for food. Though Thomas Lincoln tried to persuade his son to take up the shotgun once more, Abraham refused. He never wanted to hunt or fish again.

Nevertheless, Abraham was willing and capable of handling other chores his father asked him to do. He helped cut trees, clear fields of stumps so crops could be planted, split logs into fence rails with a heavy ax, and begin a carpenter trade in the lonely community. Despite his youth, Abraham accepted an adult workload and gave every ounce of strength and energy he had to his responsibilities.

That same year, Thomas and Elizabeth Sparrow, who were relatives of Nancy, joined the Lincoln family in Little Pigeon Creek. They brought with them their adopted son, young Dennis Hanks, whose real mother was of one of Nancy's aunts. Though Dennis was nineteen, he could not read or write, but his nature was sunny and kind. He and Abraham, despite their age difference, played together in their few spare minutes. Dennis especially adored Nancy Lincoln, but did not care much for Thomas Lincoln. In fact, his dislike of Thomas was so great that in later years he told anyone who asked him that Thomas Lincoln was lazy — a description that was far from the truth.

Life in the Indiana wilderness was often difficult and dangerous. In the summer of 1818, when Abraham was nine years old, many settlers and their animals died from a disease they called milk sickness. Thomas and Elizabeth Sparrow caught it and died, and soon afterward, Nancy came down with the fever as well.

Abraham knew almost at once that his mother was dying. She called her children to her and told them in a labored whisper to be good to one another. Then,

15

at the age of thirty-six, Nancy Lincoln died. Abraham was heartbroken and more lonely than he had ever been before. Orphaned cousin Dennis Hanks moved into the Lincoln cabin, and Abraham's eleven-year-old sister Sarah became responsible for the household. She tried hard to look after the family, but Sarah was too young to do all the chores expected of her.

Desperate to find a wife, Thomas Lincoln left young Abraham, Sarah, and Dennis alone in the little log cabin and headed back to Kentucky, returning a couple of months later with a bride. Her name was Sarah Bush Johnston. Sarah and Thomas had known one another for years. She was ten years his junior and had three children of her own. Now widowed, she needed a husband as badly as Thomas needed a wife.

Abraham loved Sarah because she quickly assumed the manner of a mother. Though there were now six children in the household, she treated them all with affection and kindness. Abraham responded eagerly to her loving ways. With the problem of the household successfully settled, Thomas turned his attention once more to the accumulation of land. The government was selling it at $1.25 per acre. Thomas bought one hundred acres and eagerly went to work.

He intended that his son should work hard, too, but Abraham had dreams of his own. Though the boy tried hard to please his father and willingly turned his hand to his daily chores, he was becoming more and more fascinated with the books he read. Abraham's books came from different sources, often borrowed from neighbors or obtained in the general stores springing up in the area. His stepmother Sarah

16

also made efforts to acquire books for him. Abraham's continuing education became important to her because she believed he could make something of himself with the proper education.

Abraham found himself especially fascinated by books which told the lives of America's founders. His favorite was Parson Weems's biography of George Washington. The parson was the first writer to set down Washington's life story, and was eager to hold up the first president as an example to children. Weems invented the story about how young George Washington chopped down the cherry tree, then told the truth to his father and bravely accepted his punishment. Abraham borrowed the biography of Washington from a neighboring farmer, and as was his habit, read it hungrily by the light of a candle late at night. As always, he stored the book between two logs in the cabin wall before settling down to sleep.

One such night there was a heavy rainstorm, and the book was soaked by the time Abraham found it in the morning. He was horrified to find a wet and almost ruined book, but the message of young Washington's honesty had inspired him. Abraham visited the farmer, told him the truth about what had happened to his book, and offered to work for the man until the book was paid for. The farmer agreed, and Abraham spent three days working in his fields. At the end of the third day, the farmer gave Abraham the Weems biography. Even as a boy, Lincoln was learning to make the right choice.

Young Abraham loved the book, and he also savored the accounts of the military campaigns waged in the American Revolutionary War. With his vivid imagination, Abraham could easily picture the colonial soldiers playing the fife and drum, the minutemen dressed in homespun uniforms carrying their muskets, and the roar of battle. Though Abraham was developing a fine sense of humor and a talent for storytelling, his passionate spirit and inventiveness set him apart from other boys. Abraham Lincoln was inspired when he conjured up images of George Washington, Thomas Jefferson, and Benjamin Franklin fighting for principles of freedom. The more he read, the more he began to realize that perhaps there was another way of life beyond the wilderness, a life he might become a part of.

This ambition to serve his fellow man was stimulated by more schooling. Between the ages of eleven and fifteen, Abraham managed short intervals at the "blab" school in the neighborhood. In blab school students spoke their lessons aloud so that the teacher could hear their progress. The education was skimpy at best, but Abraham finished the meager classes with the ability to read, write, and solve simple arithmetic problems. He also enjoyed composing lines of poetry. In one of his early copybooks he wrote:

> Abraham Lincoln
> his hand and pen
> he will be good but
> god knows when

Abraham continued his reading in the fields, often taking a book with him when he plowed. He also had a clear, readable handwriting, and would write letters for his neighbors and friends who could not.

By the age of sixteen Abraham did a man's work in the fields, but the relationship between him and his father had grown increasingly difficult. Thomas could not understand the son who yearned after the written word, and dreamed of an altogether different life. Abraham did not understand his father's willingness to settle for a limited education and a torturous life spent carving a living out of the wilderness.

Abraham had little understanding of girls, as well. Painfully aware that his tall, gawky body and sharp features repelled young ladies, he kept his distance from them. He preferred the company of men with whom he could swap stories and joke at his ease. For Abraham, girls did nothing except make him uncomfortable. He was prone to fits of unexplainable unhappiness, which frightened many girls away. Abraham was too shy to flirt with them and settled for joking uneasily when he found himself in their company. He never willingly sought out a girl as a friend.

Despite young Abraham's feeling that there must be a life somewhere that held greater rewards, he did his household tasks without resentment. At least for the time being, he knew that pleasing his father and helping to earn the family bread was his role. Abraham Lincoln knew it was the right thing to do.

3

Doing a Man's Work

IN 1828 THE world began to grow bigger for Abraham, who had reached the age of nineteen. That was the year that he found his first job away from his family. By this time, however, he was no stranger to labor for hire. His father had often lent Abraham's services to neighbors on a daily or weekly basis. Young Abraham became skillful at every kind of pioneer labor, including farming, splitting rails, and taking care of the family baby.

During one of these labor-for-hire stints, Abraham accepted his daily wages from the farmer he worked for and thanked him politely before turning home. On the way, Abraham examined the coins the farmer had handed him and realized that the farmer had made a mistake. He had paid the young laborer too much for his services.

It was bitterly cold, and Abraham had worked a long, exhausting day. Valiantly he turned around and tramped several miles back to the farmer's house. Finally Abraham knocked on the farmer's door and explained why he had returned. Then he handed the farmer the exact amount he had been overpaid. It came to six cents.

Abraham loved to tell stories, make speeches, and express opinions, and he found an eager audience in the neighbors who labored in the fields with him. They would gather around him as he spoke, neglecting their own work in order to listen. No one was more enraged by this than Thomas Lincoln, who would stride into the midst of the audience and rudely snatch his son away. He often added a slap to his wayward teenager's head as a reminder to keep his mind on his work.

Thomas was also eager for Abraham to improve his carpentry skills so that his son might work side by side with him. Abraham disliked carpentry and vowed that he would never earn his living at it. Fortunately, a merchant named Gentry offered him an alternative.

James Gentry was the wealthiest man in the Little Pigeon Creek settlement. He had founded a town called Gentryville about a mile and a half from the Lincoln home, and Abraham spent all his time there when his chores were done. There he found friendship with the men who gathered in the country store. Abraham was very fond of the village blacksmith, who recited poetry and Shakespeare for his amusement, along with William Jones, the storekeeper. Eventually James Gentry and Abraham became acquainted.

By this time, stories of Abraham's physical strength were circulating freely around the area. Gentry needed a strong and capable man to accompany his son Allen on a flatboat loaded with farm goods to sell in the port city of New Orleans, Louisiana. He decided to hire Abraham, who was delighted at the prospect of floating over five hundred miles south on the Mississippi River. Lincoln had read about the historic French city of New Orleans, and now he was going to see it for himself!

Lincoln agreed to the sum of eight dollars per month as his pay for the journey. Payments would be made for each month he was away, but the money would go to his father, who was entitled to any money Abraham earned until he legally became an adult at the age of twenty-one.

The two young men set off in April 1828. The river voyage went smoothly enough until they stopped at a plantation not far from New Orleans. The boat was tied at the dock for the night, and Allen and Abraham were asleep when a band of robbers armed with clubs climbed aboard, intending to steal the cargo.

Abraham woke up at the first sounds of the intruders and grabbed a club. Though he and Allen were far outnumbered, they fought the group courageously, tossing several of the robbers into the river. He and Allen pursued the others first onto the dock and then across dry land. They returned to the boat bleeding, though not seriously wounded. Since it was possible that the intruders might return with reinforcements, Allen and Abraham hastily untied their boat from the dock and set off again in the middle of the night.

Another young man, stepping outside his familiar surroundings for the first time, might have been tempted to yield to the intruders and give them anything they wanted in order to save his life. Certainly James Gentry would not have blamed them, since he would have considered his son's life far more important than his cargo. However, Abraham could not rid himself of the idea that he had accepted a responsibility. His duties included protecting the precious cargo until they reached New Orleans. Another man might have backed down. Abraham never would.

Abraham and Allen reached New Orleans without further trouble and were impressed by its splendor. It was the largest and most exotic city he had ever seen in his life! The Creole descendants of the French and Spanish immigrants who settled New Orleans in the 1700s built houses which amazed Lincoln with their shining paint and marvelous, intricate architecture. The New Orleans women in their feathered hats, shadowy veils, and brilliant silk dresses dazzled him. He had never tasted anything like the rich, spicy Creole food that was served all along the waterfront — the fish covered in sauces of butter and garlic, and the cream-stuffed pastries. The Creole aristocrats he passed in the street spoke a delightful language he did not understand, but the sounds enchanted him as he listened.

However, Abraham and Allen remained in the city only long enough to unload and sell their cargo, and dispose of their flatboat. Having accomplished that, they caught a steamboat traveling up the Mississippi River and returned home.

The brief glimpse Abraham had of another world stayed in his mind, but he was not yet old enough to be on his own, and his family expected his help. In 1828, his older sister Sarah died while giving birth to a stillborn child. Now Abraham was Thomas's only living offspring.

A year last, in 1829, the Lincolns prepared for another move — this time to Illinois. Abraham eagerly awaited his twenty-first birthday, the momentous occasion that would release him from his father's constant criticism. But in mid-February 1830, when the Lincolns left Indiana, Abraham went with them. He was entrusted to drive one of the ox-drawn carts carrying the family's household possessions. Behind them they left the graves of Abraham's mother, his sister Sarah and her child, and Thomas and Elizabeth Sparrow. Ahead, the Lincolns faced another wilderness. Abraham, now twenty-one, eagerly looked forward to his freedom.

Even at the moment of Abraham's coming of age, he remembered the obligations he had toward his family. In his last shopping expedition at William Jones's store, he bought a small supply of pins, needles, buttons, tinware, suspenders, and knickknacks of all sorts. He intended to sell them on his way to Illinois, the money he would make would be helpful to his family. As always, Abraham was thinking of the right thing to do. The family settled in Macon County, Illinois, and Abraham dutifully helped to split the logs that fashioned the Lincolns' new cabin. They had arrived in the middle of Illinois's worst winter, so Abraham remained with his family for one more year.

In 1831, as the snow melted and the fields began to warm with the coming of spring, Abraham's thoughts returned to his own future. Once again he hired himself out as a boatman. This time his employer was a trader named Denton Offutt. Offutt had chosen Abraham and his two stepbrothers to serve as crewmen for the boat trip to New Orleans. Offutt intended to join them later in Springfield, Illinois.

Offutt met his young crew in Springfield, as promised, but he confessed when they arrived that he had been unable to hire a boat for them to take to New Orleans. So Abraham found himself and his two stepbrothers penniless and without friends in Springfield. The young men were in a difficult financial situation, so to make money they agreed to work for Offutt to hew timber from the trees and fashion their own boat for the trip to New Orleans. Offutt paid them each twelve dollars a month, and the young men carried out their part of the bargain. When the boat was finished, they set sail for New Orleans, as they had originally agreed to do.

Offutt believed that Abraham could amount to something if given the opportunity, so he offered the young man a position as clerk in a store in the small village of New Salem. The job, Offutt promised, would be waiting for him when Abraham returned from New Orleans. Lincoln's family had moved again, this time to Coles County, Illinois, and he was excited to strike out on his own. When Abraham returned from

Abraham Lincoln was born February 12, 1809 in a log cabin in Kentucky. A tall, strong young man, Lincoln worked chopping wood, earning him the nickname "Rail Splitter." This picture is based on a 1902 painting by C.M. Coolidge

New Orleans, eager to begin work, he found that once again, Offutt had offered a job that did not exist. The merchandise Offutt planned to sell had not yet arrived, leaving Abraham without work.

Resourceful as always, Abraham found a job as a clerk at the election board, checking off the names of voters as they came in to mark their ballots. However, time often lagged during the voting, and Abraham, as usual, entertained those waiting by telling yarns. One of his favorites was the lizard story.

A Baptist preacher dressed in coarse, loose clothing came to preach at the neighborhood meetinghouse. He stood at the pulpit and announced, "I am the Christ, whom I shall represent today." As the preacher began his sermon, a little blue lizard ran up his leg underneath his baggy pants. The preacher didn't want to interrupt his sermon, so he slapped at his pants, hoping to dislodge the lizard. The lizard, however, merely crawled higher and higher, until it reached the sash of his pants. The preacher loosened the piece of cloth and threw it off, but the lizard was now crawling higher and higher. The tormented preacher finally threw off his shirt.

The congregation sat horrified for a moment, until an old lady stood up and called out, "If you represent Christ, then I'm done with the Bible!"

Yarns such as these amused the voters and the others hanging around at the election board, so when Offutt's merchandise finally reached New Salem, Abraham was already warmly welcome there. For Offutt, this was a stroke of good luck, for he was a heavy drinker and often left the management of the store in Abraham's capable hands. Offutt was so pleased with Abraham's work that he boasted about him all over the county. He bragged particularly of Abraham's physical strength. Offutt claimed that the tall, gangly clerk could beat any man in the county in any contest that would involve sheer muscle. This boast came to the ears of a group of young men living in Clary's Grove, a few miles from New Salem. They were the roughest fellows for miles around, though they were surprisingly tenderhearted to those who were sick or in trouble.

The leader of this gang, Jack Armstrong, challenged Abraham to a wrestling match. Abraham strongly objected to this kind of contest, but at last he gave in. By now he was six feet four inches tall and weighed almost two hundred pounds. Abraham proved to be a formidable opponent, his strength and coordination sharpened by long years of swinging an ax. When he faced Jack Armstrong at the wrestling site, Abraham looked unbeatable.

Jack Armstrong, however, had no intention of losing, even if it meant that he had to win by cheating. For the first part of the match, he tried hard to throw Offutt's young clerk to the ground by using illegal holds and underhanded methods. Abraham, angry that the rules of the wrestling match were being ignored, accused Armstrong of cheating. This caused the entire gang from Clary's Grove to jump on Abraham's back. He threw them off and offered to fight all of them — one at a time. The spectators grew quiet as Lincoln and Armstrong wrestled each other to the ground. Abraham's face was red from the strain, and sweat poured from his forehead. His thick hair kept falling into his eyes as he circled grimly, his opponent swinging at him. Behind Abraham's dark eyes was deadly determination. No man who cheated was going to beat him!

Finally, as Armstrong wavered, Abraham lifted him by his throat and shook him until he was dizzy. The boys from Clary's Grove were subdued, and Armstrong, to his credit, shook Lincoln's hand and said admiringly that Abraham had great courage. From then on, Jack Armstrong and the young men from Clary's Grove remained faithful Lincoln followers.

Though Abraham enjoyed the company of the Clary's Grove boys and valued their friendship, he did not copy their habits. Since early on in his life, Abraham refused to drink alcoholic beverages, a behavior that puzzled many who met him later. Hard fighting and hard drinking were common among the frontiersmen, and Abraham's refusal to join them for a drink would have hurt his social standing had his other qualities been less than admirable. Once again, Lincoln did what he thought was right.

But by the end of Abraham's first year in New Salem, he had established himself as a strong, courageous, hardworking, and good-natured young man. The few who questioned his views on alcohol dismissed them as harmless and eccentric.

Though respected, Lincoln, however, was still not satisfied with his life in New Salem. Despite his love of books and his eagerness to learn, he knew that he needed more education. He applied to the village schoolmaster, Mentor Graham, to teach him. Graham was startled at the request, but Abraham's willingness and interest were obvious. Graham began to teach the young man literature, poetry, history, science, and medicine. As Abraham proved himself more and more capable, Graham added higher mathematics such as geometry and trigonometry.

The schoolteacher was very pleased with his hardworking pupil, though he was concerned for the young man's health. Abraham was so enthusiastic about reviewing his lessons that he often stayed up late at night writing, reading, and solving math problems. He may have yawned over his counter at the store the next day, but he felt well satisfied with his efforts. Lincoln's newfound education gave him the confidence to achieve a higher goal. He wanted to run for political office.

Abraham Lincoln first entered politics when he ran for office in the Illinois state legislature.

By this time, there were only two American political parties: the Whigs and the Democrats. The old Federalist party, which was favored by President George Washington, had gradually become the Whig party. The Democrats were followers of President Andrew Jackson. The Democratic-Republican party, once led by President Thomas Jefferson, had completely died out.

The Whig party believed in a strong, centralized, or federal, government that could manage trade, banking, and transportation matters of all the states. The Democrats, by contrast, believed that the individual states should govern their own affairs without interference from the federal government. Lincoln believed, as did the Whigs, that a strong federal government that made and enforced laws for all the American states was the right way to run the country, so he became a Whig candidate for the legislature. Before Lincoln could begin to campaign seriously for the legislature, however, the Black Hawk Indian War erupted.

Northwestern Illinois had been Indian territory until 1804, when the Indians deeded the land to the United States government, on the condition that they would be permitted to live there for as long as the government owned it. When white settlers began to move in, conflicts arose between the two groups.

Finally, in 1832, Chief Black Hawk crossed the river boundary of the disputed territory with five hundred Indians. Though he insisted they were there simply to plant corn, every man with him was armed. A trigger-happy soldier fired on the Indians, and the Illinois governor called for volunteers to drive the Indians back.

Abraham enlisted immediately for the necessary thirty-day period. His company consisted mainly of his friends and neighbors, and Abraham found himself swiftly elected captain. To the end of his life, he asserted that this honor was the greatest he had ever known, even though he and his men saw no action whatsoever. About the only incident that occurred during those first thirty days was when an old Indian, alone and unarmed, wandered into their camp one day by mistake. The Indian carried a letter from United States General Cass stating that he was friendly to white men, but Abraham's company didn't care. They had enlisted to kill Indians, hadn't they? Wasn't he an Indian?

Abraham swiftly took over and insisted the men hold their fire. Some of the volunteers called him a coward. Abraham replied by offering to fight any of them — then and there. But there was no need. The Clary's Grove boys, who knew just how courageous Abraham was, stood up for him. With their added strength on Abraham's side, the other volunteers unwillingly gave in.

Abraham re-enlisted twice more after his thirty days expired. In all the time he marched and snapped orders, Lincoln and his men never once saw action, not even a skirmish. When asked about his military service later, he only joked that he had had some bloody battles with mosquitoes and made charges on wild onions.

The only real effect of the Black Hawk Indian War on Abraham's career was that he returned to New Salem with only two and half weeks left to campaign for political office in the state legislature. With so little time, he could do almost nothing to make himself known to voters outside the vicinity of his home. Though he won almost every vote in New Salem, he was badly beaten in the race, and went home vowing to try again.

4

First Love and Legal Career

WITH HIS POLITICAL career stalled — at least temporarily — Lincoln had to find a way to earn his living. At the beginning of 1832 Lincoln turned twenty-three. Once more he looked for a clerk's position, but found no offers. However, a man named Rowan Herndon sold Lincoln his half-interest in his store, and Abraham suddenly advanced from hired clerk to merchant. Lincoln's partner was a man named William Berry. They bought new merchandise on credit instead of using cash, and waited to prosper.

Unfortunately, the business did not prosper. Much of the inventory bought from other merchants consisted of liquor, which Lincoln did not display or make any effort to sell. Nothing Berry said could change his attitude.

One day, Lincoln was approached by a traveler selling all kinds of odds and ends, among them an old barrel. Lincoln bought the barrel for fifty cents without even looking inside and some time later, he examined it and found on the bottom a complete set of Blackstone's *Commentaries on the Laws of England*. At that time, Blackstone was the standard text studied by lawyers in preparation for a law practice. Fascinated by his discovery, Lincoln began to read the books hungrily, and found himself increasingly interested in the legal problems he read about. *Someday,* he told himself, *I will be a lawyer.*

Though interesting, the law books did not help Lincoln's endeavors as a merchant. Lincoln and his partner Berry could not save their sinking business. Around March 1833, Lincoln sold his interest in the store to Berry, who promised to give Lincoln his money soon. Unfortunately, Berry died before he could pay his debt, and Lincoln was left penniless. To make matters worse, Lincoln owed his creditors the enormous sum of $1,100. Horrified but determined to make good on the debt, Lincoln approached all the men who had loaned him money. In his straightforward manner, he explained what had happened and asked for time to repay them. If they would be good enough not to bother him for the money, he would work hard and reimburse them all. Knowing that Lincoln was honest, hardworking, and trustworthy, the men agreed. Repaying that debt took Lincoln the better part of seventeen years.

Once more, Abraham had to seek employment. This time there was a mountain of debt on his head, a debt he was determined to lessen with every dollar he earned. He was poor and often hungry, and there was no work for a clerk, so Lincoln once again made use of his physical strength to earn a day's pay.

Lincoln could have left New Salem to seek better conditions elsewhere, but he was a man who stood by his word. He had promised to pay his debts in New Salem, and he would not leave until he had done so. Lincoln knew from his mother's teachings that Providence would lead him to his chosen career when the time was right. He turned out to be correct.

In May 1833, at the age of twenty-four, Lincoln was appointed postmaster of New Salem, Illinois. Though working in the post office allowed Lincoln to send personal letters without charge and entitled him to one daily newspaper free, the young postmaster found many of the government's rules bothersome. But when someone was particularly eager to receive a letter, Lincoln would walk several miles in any kind of weather to deliver it personally. He began to carry such letters and documents under his high silk stovepipe hat, and the habit remained with him all his life. Even as president, Lincoln continued to carry keys, letters, and small items on his thick hair under his hat.

In addition, as postmaster, young Lincoln saw all the newspapers that were published in that part of the country. The news was often fascinating and informative. He began reading daily newspapers; a habit that continued for the rest of his life.

Anxious to increase his earnings, Lincoln looked about for other jobs that he could do in his spare time. He only earned about twenty-five dollars a year as postmaster, and he needed additional income, so

he sought out work writing neighbors' letters, splitting rails, working at the mill, and harvesting in the
fields.

Lincoln also secured the post of deputy surveyor
to John Calhoun, who was the surveyor for the
county. Because he knew nothing about surveying,
Lincoln turned to his old schoolmaster, Mentor Graham, for help. Lincoln and Graham worked together
night after night, studying two textbooks on surveying. By the end of the year, Lincoln knew the books
thoroughly, had bought a horse, and presented himself to Calhoun, ready to start work.

Lincoln was considered so trustworthy that many
people asked him to draw up simple legal documents
for the sale of their land. Since Lincoln was now working at surveying, he had a knowledge of land bound-
aries and an understanding of how to word a
contract. People trusted him to handle their affairs
carefully and honestly, and they nicknamed him
"Honest Abe." Lincoln always appreciated the tribute to his honesty, but until the end of his life, he
detested the nickname Abe, and preferred always to
call himself Abraham.

Despite all his hard work, Lincoln managed to
spend time with his neighbors as well. James Rutledge, an innkeeper, one of the men to whom Lincoln
was in debt, found the young man very appealing.
So did his attractive young daughter Ann, one of the
best-loved girls in New Salem. She was kind and very
beautiful, but she was engaged to another man. Lincoln was contented to talk with her as a friend,
though he was moved by the gentle look in her lovely

blue eyes. Ann's fiancé took a journey east to visit his father and other relatives in New York. He expected to return in a short time and marry his sweetheart Ann. In the meantime, Lincoln enjoyed his own quiet visits with Ann Rutledge.

Though Lincoln's heart held him in New Salem, his mind was firmly looking ahead. In August 1834 he once more ran for the legislature. This time, with more time to campaign, he won the election for the Whig party. At last, Abraham Lincoln's political career had begun at the age of twenty-five.

The position of state assemblyman required that Lincoln take up residence in Vandalia, Illinois's capital until 1839. The legislature convened in early December and closed its session at the end of February. So in November 1834, Abraham Lincoln, freshly attired in a crisp new suit from a Springfield tailor, rode the stagecoach to Vandalia.

Before he had left, a farmer named Coleman Smoot lent Lincoln $200 to buy new clothes and help settle some of his outstanding debts before he left New Salem. He also needed to find lodgings in Vandalia and buy his meals, and he had no money to pay for these until the legislators voted themselves a partial payment on their salaries in December.

Lincoln, a little overwhelmed by his new surroundings, rented a small room at the Vandalia Inn. Though Lincoln had visited New Orleans for a short time many years before, New Salem had been the most bustling town he had lived in up to that point. Vandalia offered so much activity that he was a little dazed.

Despite the charm of the town, Lincoln himself lived in poverty. His room at the Vandalia Inn was tiny, dark, and furnished only with the barest necessities. Lincoln further cut down on expenses by dining as simply as possible. To another man, these living conditions might have been disheartening. To Lincoln, who had lived in poverty all his life, it was the only way to save enough money to pay off his remaining debt.

Lincoln's attention was completely focused on his new job in the legislature as its session convened. Like many young politicians, Lincoln spent his first term mostly listening to more experienced assemblymen, memorizing tricks of oration, examining the bills they wrote, and asking questions.

Perhaps the most important of his new acquaintances was Stephen A. Douglas. Though younger than Lincoln, Douglas had already planned to occupy the office of state attorney. Lincoln was a little startled at this brashness, especially since Douglas had only moved from Vermont to Illinois the year before. But the Little Giant, as Douglas later became known, would battle Lincoln fiercely for several political offices — and even in courting the same woman. At the moment, though, Lincoln paid little attention to the inexperienced young man from Vermont. He was too busy watching and listening to politicians whose experience he respected and whom he hoped to follow someday. When the legislative session was over in February, he journeyed back to New Salem, anxious once more to see the delicate and warm Ann Rutledge.

Ann's expected marriage had not taken place because her fiancé had not returned from his New York trip. Though he had faithfully written to her, the letters became fewer and fewer, and the excuses for his absence were longer and less believable. Ann, lonely and bewildered by the silence of her fiance, was glad to see and chat with her friend Abraham Lincoln.

As time passed, Ann and Abraham spent more and more of their days together. He had worked hard while serving in his first term at Vandalia and needed to rest and clear his mind before the next session of the legislature began. Finally, Ann realized that the man who loved her was the man by her side, not the man who had gone away and had failed to return. She wrote to McNamar, asking him to release her from her promise to marry him. When no answer came, she knew she had made the right choice.

The path of Abraham and Ann seemed very clear. She would attend an academy for young ladies in Jacksonville in the fall. Abraham, her new fiancé, would return to Vandalia and continue to work toward paying off his mountain of debt. Then they would marry. Once again, Providence stepped into Lincoln's life. In the late summer of 1835, malaria, a sickness carried by mosquitoes, descended on New Salem. The wilderness settlers expected the fevers, so regularly did they appear. First Lincoln caught the sickness and struggled against the cycles of chills and fever, but in a few weeks, he was back on his feet. Unfortunately, Ann was not that strong, and in a short time she was gravely ill.

Finally her family called for Lincoln, who rode out to their farm and sat with the delirious young woman, her lovely auburn hair now drenched with sweat from the high fever. He sat with her, alone, for two days, until her eyes closed for the last time. Lincoln's first sweetheart and the great love of his life was dead. When her funeral was over, Lincoln was dazed with grief. The one woman he'd believed could love and understand him was gone, and he could not imagine ever finding her equal.

Lincoln's friends could usually count on him to be cheerful and sunny, but not now. Instead they saw a man sinking into a deep depression, and they tried desperately to help. The village doctor recommended rest, so Lincoln obediently went to the home of friends. They allowed him to help with the chores, as he had chosen, but wisely kept their silence. Lincoln was in no mood to talk.

Many weeks passed before Lincoln began to recover from his despair. The friends who saw him through this period always insisted that when Ann died, something died in Lincoln as well. The painful memory of her remained as a shadow in his eyes for the rest of his life.

Lincoln returned to Vandalia in the fall for his second legislative session, and this time was a more active participant. He was interested in the bills introduced for the improvement of roads and canals in the state and voted for them all. When the time came for him to run for re-election in 1836, he retained his seat in an easy victory and became the Whig floor leader.

In 1837 Lincoln made his first public statement on slavery. Lincoln and another legislator filed protest against a resolution that failed to call slavery an evil practice. Together they declared, "the institution of slavery is founded on both injustice and bad policy."

Lincoln's personal life could not stop altogether, even though his true love was gone. A year after Ann's death, Lincoln met Mrs. Bennett Able, a married woman he had known for some time. She had been raised in Kentucky and was about to travel there to visit her family. Her sister, Mary Owens, was still unmarried, so Mrs. Able proposed to bring her back to Illinois, if Lincoln would agree to court Mary and eventually marry her.

In a moment of recklessness, Lincoln agreed. He remembered Mary from her visit to Illinois a few years before, but when she arrived he was shocked at her appearance. She had grown stout and was not as attractive as he had remembered. Lincoln had given his word, and therefore must honor the bargain he had struck. He believed it was the right thing to do.

Lincoln began to court Mary, dutifully writing her letters while he was in Vandalia. His enthusiasm, however, was nowhere near what he had experienced with Ann Rutledge. In addition, Lincoln feared that his poverty in Vandalia would come as a rude shock to Mary, who had been raised in comfortable surroundings. If she loved him deeply, the poverty would be of no consequence, but Lincoln rather suspected that she did not feel that strongly toward him.

Finally, after an eight-month courtship, he put the matter to her plainly. Would she be happy under the

41

circumstances he could offer her? If she would be, he would stick to his bargain. If not, she should think seriously about withdrawing from what might become a most painful situation.

Mary Owens's answer was apparently satisfactory, for he continued to court her. When he finally proposed marriage, she gave him a powerful surprise. Her answer was no. Determined, Abraham pursued Mary and asked her again. The answer remained the same. Her rejection was most puzzling for he had considered that she was attractive to no one but himself, yet she had refused to share his life. Lincoln concluded that he would never be able to attract a worthwhile woman to accept his name and his fate. He withdrew his proposal of marriage from Mary Owens so that he could concentrate on his career.

At the age of twenty-eight Lincoln was ready to leave New Salem. Certainly no place had ever offered him more opportunity or made him realize what he could achieve. He left the little village with far more than he had brought to it. His new home, he determined, would be the thriving town of Springfield, Illinois.

Lincoln's study of the lawbooks he bought and borrowed made it possible for him to apply to the Circuit Court of Sangamon County for admission to the bar. No formal study or examination was required then to become a lawyer. Lincoln brought letters to the county clerk guaranteeing his honesty, and recited an oath to support the Constitution of the United States. The county clerk was satisfied. Abraham Lincoln was now considered an attorney at law.

John T. Stuart, a longtime friend and respected attorney, offered the new lawyer an opportunity to join his practice. Their firm became Stuart and Lincoln. Lincoln worked hard for his clients, but if one of them proved to be guilty of a crime, Lincoln's principles would often overshadow his legal expertise. He had no heart to defend the guilty. Yet no one was a more eloquent champion of the poor and the unjustly accused than Abraham Lincoln.

Lincoln never failed to display his sense of honor as an attorney. When his partner went to Washington for a term in Congress, Lincoln continued to run the firm with skill and hard work. When Stuart returned, after exchanging news, Lincoln rose and stuck his hand into a cubbyhole in the cherry-colored desk they both used. It contained packages of money, neatly labeled in Lincoln's hand, and represented Stuart's earnings as an attorney during his term in Congress. Lincoln had faithfully saved every penny and duly turned it over to his partner.

5

Marriage and Family Life

STEPHEN DOUGLAS BECAME even better known to Lincoln as the years rolled on. Douglas was now a prosecuting attorney in Springfield, Illinois and often faced Lincoln in the courtroom. Like Lincoln, he was a spellbinding orator. The little man used a booming voice to carry his points, whereas the tall, lanky frontiersman with the high-pitched voice spoke as though he were addressing friends around the dinner table.

The political differences between Lincoln and Douglas automatically set them at opposite poles. Lincoln was a Whig who believed in a strong centralized government. Douglas was a Democrat who supported his party's belief in the rights of individual states to govern themselves. Since they each kept seats in the legislature, their glaring clash of opinions began to make itself felt.

Lincoln and Douglas were rivals in personal matters, as well. By 1839, at the age of thirty, Lincoln was practicing law with confidence. His frontier days were behind him, he thought. Though his accent still spoke of the backwoods, he had spent many years patiently educating himself and studying the manners and conversation of men far more polished and sophisticated. He believed himself to be the equal of the men he met, both in the legislature and the courtroom.

However, in 1839 Lincoln's confidence was severely tested when he met Mary Todd, the woman who would eventually become his wife. She had been born to a wealthy banking family in Kentucky and had long been accustomed to the best of everything. She was twenty-one, ten years Lincoln's junior. Mary was a spirited and intelligent woman who often appeared at the best Springfield parties and dances. Unlike Lincoln, she was vivacious and at ease at social functions, and very soon she was considered one of the most popular Southern belles of the town.

Although Mary was raised and educated in Kentucky, her beliefs were not completely Southern. She had grown up with slaves in her home, but the adult Mary Todd had come to believe in the abolition of slavery.

As a child, Mary had observed her Negro nanny handing food hurriedly to slaves fleeing the South through the Underground Railroad. The Underground Railroad was a network of people who would shelter and feed runaway slaves as they made their way north to freedom. Mary believed that helping slaves escape was morally right and should be encouraged. She also

45

knew that it was a dangerous activity, so she never mentioned it to her parents.

A few years later, when she was in Kentucky, Mary had watched a slave auction that left her with vivid memories of the horrors of slavery. She was no stranger to slave auctions, but this one was of particular interest. One of the young women to be auctioned was only one sixty-fourth black in her ancestry, yet this was considered enough to brand her a slave.

The teenager had a complexion as fair as Mary's and had been raised as white until that moment. Mary felt as though one of her friends was being sold into slavery and watched, horrified, as the auctioneer displayed the young woman, shouting her fine qualities to the crowd of slave buyers watching and bidding. At that moment Mary began to understand the injustice of slavery for all people.

This was normal procedure during a slave auction, but seeing this person treated in such a manner angered Mary. She was very relieved then, when the winning bid came from a minister who announced loudly that he would free the slave at once. From that time forward, Mary supported the abolition of slavery. She realized that no one, black or white, should be a slave.

In 1839 Mary Todd was courted by several young men, many of whom were interested in political careers. Her father had been fascinated by politics and mingled freely with political figures in Kentucky, among them Henry Clay, one of Lincoln's great heroes. When she mentioned her father's interest in politics to Abraham, she was surprised to see a flicker of interest in his eyes.

Mary understood Lincoln's ambitions, as she understood the goals of Stephen Douglas, who also came to woo her. She jokingly told her sister Elizabeth that she intended to marry a man who would someday be president.

Certainly, the society people with whom Mary spent time encouraged that ambition. Mary's sister and brother-in-law, however, found little to recommend in Lincoln. In fact, they strongly objected to him. His upbringing and education could scarcely be compared with Mary's. The match could not possibly bring either of them any happiness. How could she even consider such a gawky, awkward man when men like Stephen Douglas were calling on her?

Mary, however, soon felt she could never truly be happy with a man like Douglas, and her interest in Lincoln's courtship intensified. Throughout 1840 they saw each other quite often, and finally an engagement was announced. Their wedding date was set for January 1, 1841.

To everyone's surprise, Lincoln failed to show up for his own wedding. He suffered an extreme attack of depression, doubting his ability to bring happiness to a woman he loved. He knew he could bear poverty; he was certainly used to it. But Mary Todd had no idea what poverty was. Every wish she had ever asked for had been instantly granted. She had even admitted that she could not understand why newly married couples suddenly became so somber. For all of Mary's education, wit, and charm, her protected upbringing had kept her very childlike.

Lincoln's own fear of failure and his lack of confidence in his own worth as a husband were the real factors that caused him to back away from the marriage ceremony. This depression did not fade away, as it had after Ann Rutledge's death. Though Lincoln knew he had hurt Mary, he felt that their marriage would only bring her unhappiness.

At the same time, Abraham's close friend Joshua Speed was also courting a young woman he hoped to marry. Though Lincoln did not believe in marital happiness for himself, he urged Speed to marry the lady of his choice. When Speed objected, wondering if he could really be happy, Lincoln insisted he would be.

Three months after his wedding, Speed declared himself to be the happiest of men, and tried to persuade Lincoln that his own happiness could be greatly increased by marriage. Soon afterward, Mary and Lincoln met once again, accidentally, at the home of a mutual friend.

This first meeting led to more contact and a renewal of their courtship. This time Lincoln's mind was at ease. His friend had set a good example. Once more he proposed marriage, and Mary accepted. They were married quietly on November 4, 1842. At the age of thirty-three, Abraham Lincoln had finally found a wife.

Mary was in for many surprises about marriage. Lincoln's New Salem debts still absorbed most of his income, and the couple were forced to live in a room at the Globe Tavern in Springfield, where lodging cost only four dollars a week.

Mary tried to conceal her feelings about living in the dank, ugly room, but she fretted that her wealthier friends would not call on them in such a place. Only a few months after the wedding, she became pregnant. Mary could have returned to her sister's comfortable home when the baby was due, but she was stubborn. Though she hated the room at the Globe Tavern, she stayed there and gave birth to Robert Todd Lincoln on August 1, 1843.

Though Lincoln was able to provide a house a year later, Mary never recovered from her plunge into poverty and became frightened of their humble living conditions. Because her traditional Southern upbringing had not prepared her for this humble life-style, she had little training in how to plan a family budget, buy food for meals, or handle crying children. The life she had prepared for — one of wealth, ease, and much entertaining with many servants — was not the life she had chosen.

When he was at home, Abraham often helped to care for his new son, but just as often he was out riding the law circuit. He traveled to the circuit courts wherever they were set up and tried his law cases there. At one point Lincoln's circuit included fifteen counties and covered about 8,000 square miles. With this heavy workload, he could be away for several weeks or months at a time. This only increased Mary's jumpiness. Even so, at this time in his life, Abraham Lincoln felt well satisfied with marriage. He knew that a home with a family he loved would help him in the stormy sea of politics.

6

Entering National Politics

B Y 1845 THE Lincoln family was living in a modest but comfortable home. Now Lincoln's thoughts turned to national politics. He wanted to win the Whig party nomination to the United States Congress, but the Whigs in his home county were supporting Lincoln's good friend Edward Baker. To further dampen Lincoln's spirits, they elected him as a delegate to the convention which nominated Baker. Lincoln said sadly that it was the equivalent of being the best man at the wedding when the groom is marrying your sweetheart. Nevertheless, Lincoln accepted the loss gracefully because that was the right thing to do.

Never one to allow defeat to set him back, Lincoln decided that the time had come for him to leave his present job as a junior law partner and establish his own law firm. Lincoln chose William Herndon as his new partner, a young lawyer who was dedicated to the abolition of slavery.

With his new law firm set up, and his partner taking care of the bookkeeping, Lincoln was able to pursue his goal of being elected to the United States Congress. He was elected to Congress in 1847, at the age of thirty-eight.

When Lincoln took his seat in Congress in December, the war between the United States and Mexico was causing everyone great concern. Texas had become a state in 1845, but Mexico still claimed it as her territory.

On his second day in Congress, Lincoln heard President Polk assert that the Mexican army had fired on Americans. Lincoln was convinced that Polk was mistaken about the hostilities in Mexico, so a few days later Lincoln introduced a resolution, which embarrassed Polk. Lincoln's resolutions forced the president to admit that America had been the aggressor in the war, that the first bloodshed occurred not on American soil, as Polk claimed, but on Mexican soil. Three weeks later Lincoln spoke for the first time on the floor of the Congress.

Lincoln's eloquent speech contained many facts and specific charges. He insisted that the Mexicans were correct in claiming certain land as their own — land that the Texans also claimed. Lincoln pleaded for peace with Mexico.

The reaction to Lincoln's speech was one of surprise. No one realized that this mild-looking man had such force and conviction. Although his speech was eloquent, criticism of his opinions began to circulate because he had broken Illinois's patriotic viewpoint. Residents of Illinois began to call him Benedict Arnold, after the famous traitor of the American Revolution. Abraham Lincoln was called a coward.

Lincoln tried to defend himself by sending copies of statements of other Whigs who shared his opinions to newspapers, but the editors refused to print them. As a result, when his term was up he did not receive another nomination. Another freshman congressman would have spent his term listening, offering no opinion that would conflict with those of his party. Lincoln could not sit quietly. Even if it meant losing his chance for a second term in Congress, he felt honor bound to speak out for what he believed was right.

The issue of slavery was becoming a hot political issue as well. Lincoln favored the abolition of slavery. But he was more concerned with how ending slavery would affect the two halves of the country, the North and the South.

The states of the North had grown swiftly into an industrial community, employing hundreds of thousands of men in factories, ironworks, and shipyards. Skilled immigrants from European countries, seeking fresh opportunity, often landed in New York or Boston. They were willing to labor for low wages, and the Northern employers gladly hired them. The South, on the other hand, was an agricultural community. Farming was the primary source of income, and large numbers of unskilled laborers were absolutely necessary to work in the fields. The skilled immigrants remained in the North, leaving only slave labor to harvest Southern crops and work in Southern households.

Lincoln feared that abolishing slavery in one swift stroke might destroy the South economically. Where would they find labor to replace the slaves who cost them so little? How could they continue to grow and harvest their crops without slaves? This was a serious problem that had to be solved.

Lincoln's thoughts also turned to the Whig nominee for president, General Zachary Taylor, who had won great popularity during the Mexican War in 1846. Though Lincoln was against the war, he campaigned fervently for Taylor and was pleased to see him nominated at the Whig National Convention in Philadelphia.

Taylor won the presidency, but his victory only pointed out to Lincoln the failure of his own efforts. Lincoln had gone to Congress with the good wishes of his friends, but he had left disappointed and bitterly resented by many of his own supporters. He saw no path open to him other than taking up his law practice once more.

During this time, Lincoln's family was growing — and grieving. His second son, Edward had been born in 1846, but at the age of four he fell ill. Mary and Abraham nursed him frantically for two months, but he died on February 1, 1850.

Mary collapsed completely. Lincoln tried to support her and help her, but he could not bring her out of her grief, which was no less deep than his own. He watched helplessly as she reached out to a local minister, who assured her that Eddie was in heaven and happy and well. Mary desperately needed that comfort, and she began to take a new interest in religion.

To please his wife, Lincoln bought a pew at church where she could go to pray as often as she liked.

The birth of William Lincoln only eleven months later was a much-needed break from grief. But at the same time, Lincoln's father Thomas was gravely ill. Less than a month after the birth of his grandson, Lincoln's father died.

In 1853 Mary gave birth to another son, whom they named Thomas Lincoln, for Abraham's father. The child's head was large, so they called him "Tad," short for tadpole. The nickname stuck, and because of the loss of their son Ed, the Lincolns often overprotected Tad. He also began to talk with a lisp, which only made his mother spoil him that much more.

Both parents encouraged their children's opinions and fancies. Willie loved railroads and memorized railroad timetables as a hobby. His proudest achievement was conducting an imaginary train from Chicago to New York without a single mistake.

Mary and Abraham took great care over their oldest son Robert's education and sent him to the best schools possible to prepare him for any career he chose. Although Robert failed his first entrance examinations to Harvard, he was determined, like his father, so he set himself to studying even harder. He intended, like his father, to triumph over every obstacle.

7

The Path to the Presidency

IN 1854, WHEN Abraham Lincoln was forty-five years old, Steven Douglas once again met him in the political arena. That was the year that Douglas introduced the Kansas-Nebraska Act in Congress. It was a bill designed to permit the two new states to decide for themselves whether or not they wanted to allow slavery within their borders.

Lincoln spoke fervently against the bill because it represented the Democratic states'-rights ideology. Lincoln disagreed with Douglas's view that neighboring states wouldn't care about the new states' status as slave or free. But the law passed and the slavery issue became even more controversial.

Naturally, Lincoln's outspoken argument brought him new enemies within his party, so he decided that the Whigs no longer represented his political viewpoint or interests. He knew there was still resentment over his speeches on the Mexican War, so when the new Republican party was born in 1854, Lincoln joined them.

The Kansas-Nebraska Act was not successful. Nebraska was not suited to a slave economy, but Kansas was. When settlers flooded into Kansas with their slaves, conflict resulted. In 1855, John Brown, a deeply religious abolitionist, led an attack on slave-owning settlers in Pottawatamie Creek, Kansas. The unarmed settlers were jerked from sleep in the middle of the night and slaughtered.

Lincoln, like many other Northern Republicans, believed that the institution of slavery had to be abolished. He worked with other Illinois men to found the Illinois branch of the Republican party, and in June 1858, he was rewarded with his party's nomination for the Senate.

Lincoln's nomination speech included these insightful words: "A house divided against itself cannot stand. I believe this government cannot endure, permanently half-slave and half-free. I do not expect the Union to be dissolved — I do not expect the house to fall — but I do expect it will cease to be divided. It will become all one thing, or all the other."

Lincoln's opponent for Senate was the Democratic nominee Stephen Douglas, "The Little Giant." Few senatorial races have ever been as hotly contested as this one. Both candidates severely criticized each other's positions on the slavery issue. They spent most of their time in front of audiences defending various charges made by the other.

Lincoln felt this was not productive or helpful to the voters. He wrote to Douglas, proposing that they debate each other on the various issues before audiences around Illinois. Douglas agreed. They met seven times in different parts of the state to discuss how they felt about the questions facing the voters. Such debates had never before occurred in the history of American politics. The 1858 Lincoln-Douglas debates provided some of Illinois's best entertainment, because the two candidates were both brilliant and persuasive speakers.

Douglas was a fiery orator who often turned the tables on his opponent, but Lincoln countered the attacks with eloquence and common sense. Douglas attacked Lincoln for his anti-slavery views. Lincoln, on the other hand, considered slavery "moral, social, and political evil."

The opponents fought verbal battles up and down the counties of Illinois. When Douglas tried to cover up his own views before a hostile audience, Lincoln retorted, "You can fool all of the people some of the time, and some of the people all of the time. But you can't fool all of the people all of the time." It remains one of Lincoln's best-known comments.

But even Lincoln's eloquence could not cool the states'-rights fever stirred up by Douglas. Douglas won the election and Lincoln was bitterly disappointed over this defeat. Once again,he had no choice but to continue to practice law and work for his party whenever possible.

The year was 1859 and opposing groups continued to fight over the slavery issue. John Brown, the abolitionist who had led the 1855 midnight massacre now led a band of men to the United States arsenal at Harpers Ferry, in what is now West Virginia. The intent was to arm the people and to set up a full-scale slave rebellion. The militia was called in to fight Brown's rebels, and it took two days to subdue them. John Brown was jailed and hanged later that year.

Then, in 1860, Lincoln got an important opportunity that would change the course of his life and the history of the United States forever. Cooper Union, an institution of higher learning, in New York City, asked Lincoln to speak about the issue of slavery, and he agreed. Most New Yorkers had never seen or heard of the lanky Illinois lawyer, and as he addressed the sophisticated crowd of men and women, he took them all by surprise.

Lincoln's words that night were so powerful, so eloquent, that New York newspapers took notice of him. The Harpers Ferry revolt had inspired Lincoln to make one of his most passionate speeches that night, which ended with this plea: "Let us have faith that right makes might, and in that faith let us to the end dare to do our duty as we understand it."

It was this first truly national coverage that led to Lincoln's nomination for president in 1860. Who was his opponent? Who else, but Senator Stephen Douglas? Lincoln could not have beaten a solid Democratic party for the presidency in 1860, but the Democratic party at that time was far from solid. The split over the slavery question provided the wedge Lincoln needed to win.

In 1860, the Democrats ran two candidates, not one as they do today: Stephen Douglas in the North and John C. Breckinridge in the South. Douglas had tried to persuade the Southern audiences that he was on their side. However, he had made speeches in the Senate that raised doubts as to his real feelings about states' rights and slavery. The South did not trust him, and he would need their votes in order to win the election. A fourth nominee was an independent named John Bell. Between the votes he won and the votes split between the two Democratic candidates, the Republicans felt confident that their candidate, Abraham Lincoln, would win.

Lincoln had the support of the entire Republican party, and he was the best candidate possible, they felt. Though his national exposure was limited, his anti-slavery views and passionate speeches persuaded many Northerners that he was the best candidate for the nation's highest office.

On election day, Lincoln waited uneasily at the telegraph office in Springfield for the results. The election results trickled in on that cold November day in 1860. Sitting with some of his Republican supporters, Lincoln listened as the vote tabulations came in from around the country. He tried to joke, but for once his words were humorless. His face showed lines of tension as the telegraph keys clicked their message. What Lincoln originally wanted was only a second term in Congress. What he might win would be the most powerful position in the country, the office of president.

The final results of the election did not come in until after midnight. Abraham Lincoln, a Republican, had won and would become the sixteenth president of the United States. Lincoln's feelings of anxiety were evident when he spoke to newspaper reporters the day after the election. "Well, boys," he said, "your troubles are over. Mine have just begun." Lincoln was right, because he would be president during America's bloodiest conflict — the Civil War.

8

The North Against the South

ALTHOUGH LINCOLN ESCAPED unharmed from the Confederate murderers in Baltimore just prior to his inauguration on March 4, 1861, the unrest in the country quickly grew worse — especially in the South.

A number of meetings had already been held in some Southern states, where cries of war were being heard. The news of Lincoln's election was the last spark Southerners needed to revolt. The state of South Carolina seceded from the Union, ten other Southern states followed, and the Confederacy was formed. This new country would govern its own affairs and have its own army to preserve its Southern traditions, including slavery. War between the states of the North and the states of the South was now inevitable.

Lincoln faced other problems, too. One of his first responsibilities was to appoint a cabinet of advisers. Many of the men Lincoln considered for important government positions had their own political goals. William Seward of New York had held presidential ambitions, but Lincoln appointed him secretary of state. Salmon Chase, who hoped to run for the presidency in 1864, was appointed secretary of the treasury.

Many of Lincoln's advisers believed him to be a soft-hearted, not-very-able administrator. Secretary of State Seward hoped to gain control of the administration by telling Lincoln what to decide on important matters of state. Fortunately, Lincoln had his own ideas about governing the country. He particularly wanted to keep the Union whole, but as the Southern states announced their secession one after another, he realized that a war between the states could not be avoided.

On April 12, 1861, barely a month after Lincoln's inauguration, the North and South began what was to become four years of bloodshed that would leave a legacy of grief and bitterness. Confederate soldiers in South Carolina watched, steely eyed, as Northern troops tried to bring food and supplies to Fort Sumter, the only Union fort left in that rebellious Southern state. Southerners raged and the Confederate soldiers opened fire. The Civil War had begun.

Curiously, there was a two-month silence before the first major battle of the war was fought. Lincoln, who had no background or experience in military matters, wanted to leave the fighting of the war to a well-trained and experienced general. His first choice was a brave Virginian named Robert E. Lee, but Lee could not bring himself to fight a war against his home state. Though he did not totally believe in the Southerners' point of

Political satire was popular in Lincoln's day, and he was a
favorite subject. This cartoon shows an ax-wielding President
Lincoln cutting down the tree of slavery in order to force
the South back into the Union

view, he resigned from the Union army and became a general in Confederate forces in 1861.

It was no secret to Northern officials in Washington that the Confederate army was poorly equipped, ill trained, and only a fraction of the size of the Union army. Lincoln was cheered by the promise of his generals and Secretary of War Simon Cameron that the war would be over in a month.

The first major confrontation between the Union and Confederate armies came on July 21, 1861 at Manassas, Virginia, in what was called the First Battle of Bull Run. There was great excitement in nearby Washington. Many civilians, not understanding the seriousness of the situation, packed picnic lunches and went to a nearby bluff to watch the fighting and enjoy the spectacle. The sound of the cannon was plainly heard in the capital. Even Lincoln's two sons Willie and Tad peered across the river with a telescope to see the unfolding battle. Lincoln paced back and forth in the telegraph office across the street from the White House, waiting for word of the outcome.

For a time, there was great optimism. Union troops appeared to be victorious, but by three o'clock in the afternoon they were in full retreat. The Union army had little training and could not follow orders efficiently. Meanwhile, Confederate soldiers fought furiously for the South. When Southern reinforcements charged in late that afternoon, the Confederates won the battle.

Lincoln was stunned at the Union army's crushing defeat, but he bowed to facts. Lincoln needed a new general, so he handed the command of the Union army to a dashing thirty-four-year-old Mexican War hero named George McClellan. In a few weeks Major General McClellan trained the Union army and had won several skirmishes in western Virginia, pushing the Confederate troops entirely out of the area. He became an instant hero in the press. Lincoln believed that General McClellan would bring swift and decisive victory to the Union, but this was not to be.

Lincoln soon learned that some of his most trusted men had plans of their own. McClellan, for example, was a Democrat, and he intended to run for president in 1864. He believed that if he could treat the South gently, he could win their votes. His strategy, therefore, was to avoid fighting the Confederate forces at all. Lincoln was bewildered when McClellan's well-trained army sat in camp or marched for miles, never engaging in battle with the enemy.

Lincoln was also becoming suspicious of Secretary of War Cameron, who was padding his own pockets through every kind of crooked maneuvering. In addition, Secretary of the Treasury Chase had issued currency with Lincoln's face on the five-dollar bill, but had himself pictured on the one-dollar bill.

As the war ground on, Lincoln's home life suffered. As his wife Mary grew older, she had begun to develop blinding headaches of such intensity that she often did not know what she was doing or saying. When the pain reached unendurable levels, she frequently fainted. Often she was sick in bed for days, unable to speak to anyone or carry out her normal daily tasks. Doctors could give her nothing to ease the pain. Lincoln spent hours with Mary during these times, talking quietly to her and waiting on her. He was the only person she would ever allow at her bedside during these bouts of agony.

At the same time, Mary was proceeding with her own plans for the Lincoln administration. She intended to redecorate the White House by replacing its faded carpets and curtains with new and expensive furnishings. She began the project with great enthusiasm, but soon found herself sinking into debt.

Throughout the war years, Mary spent money freely with no regard for her husband's income. She was the first lady, wasn't she? She felt that she was entitled to the best of everything in the country! She knew that as long as Lincoln was president, the bill collectors would not press her for payment. Once Lincoln left office, however, she did not know how to begin to pay them. At one point, Mary's own debts — for clothes, jewelry, and other personal items — rose to $27,000, a sum greater than Lincoln's yearly income as president. Mary was ashamed to tell what she had done, so she avoided the subject with him at all costs.

Perhaps to offset her extravagance with clothes and jewels, Mary insisted that the family keep a cow on the White House lawn. The cow was to provide milk for the occupants, but this unrealistic attempt at saving money was unsuccessful.

The Lincolns suffered another personal tragedy in 1862. Eleven-year-old Willie caught a fever that he could not shake off, and he was dead in a few days. Lincoln was greatly saddened by his death, but this second loss of a child shattered Mary.

Even Mary's religion could not comfort her this time, and her husband was burdened with the escalating war. Mary began to seek help from mediums and psychics, who claimed they could hold seances to restore Willie's spirit to her. From then on, Mary spent a great deal of time and money trying to communicate with Willie in the spirit world through various psychics and spiritual encounters.

Lincoln, meanwhile, poured his energy into holding together a nation that was sadly tearing itself apart. He wished fervently to keep the Union as one nation. Years before, he himself had said decisively that a house divided against itself could not stand. Now he saw the evidence daily.

To stem the tide of recent Confederate victories, Lincoln appointed a relatively unknown soldier, General Ulysses S. Grant, to command the Union armies in the West. The president was becoming impatient with General McClellan, and worried. Lincoln had deliberately downplayed his own strong views on slavery, hoping to calm Southern fears. As a compromise, he was willing to phase out slavery slowly if it would help the South's agricultural economy respond to the change. Yet the Union was not winning battles, and he felt he would have to make a strong stand against slavery in order to bolster the spirits of the fading Northern army.

Finally, on September 17, 1862, the Union army scored a decisive victory over the Confederate troops at Antietam. Lincoln expected General McClellan to give chase to the retreating Confederates, but McClellan, his own ambitions for president burning, let the rebel forces get away safely. Lincoln was outraged. He replaced McClellan with Ambrose Burnside, and within a year would replace Burnside with Joseph Hooker.

At the same time, President Lincoln had his own strategy in mind. He said, "We must change our tactics or lose the game." He proclaimed that unless the rebel states returned to the Union by January 1, 1863, he would write an order freeing the Southern slaves. The South refused to comply, and Lincoln issued the Emancipation Proclamation on New Year's Day, 1863, declaring the slaves, "forever free." But the war went on.

While the Emancipation Proclamation freed slaves only in the rebelling Southern states, it did pave the way for the Thirteenth Constitutional Amendment. This amendment, ratified in 1865, stated that slavery shall not exist in the United States and that Congress had the power to enforce this law.

Abraham Lincoln had always believed that the greatest danger to the Union was not the issue of slavery but the division of the country into two separate and weaker nations. Yet slavery was an issue that had divided the country, not united it. The Emancipation Proclamation was a decisive strategy that would boost the spirits of the brave soldiers, both black and white, fighting to preserve the Union.

President Abraham Lincoln believed in freedom for everyone in the United States — both in the North and the South. He believed that his fight to preserve the Union was the right thing to do — no matter what it cost.

9

Turning the Tide at Gettysburg

EVEN WHEN LINCOLN became president, he still clung to the habits he had established in the days when he was a store clerk. He still rose early — sometimes as early as five-thirty in the morning — and he still ate lightly. His breakfast usually consisted of a single egg, his lunch was often a single apple and one biscuit. Supper was soup, a slice of meat, and a potato. The only dessert he sampled was apple pie.

By 1863, as the war raged on into its third year, President Lincoln's thick, dark hair became peppered with gray. The beard he had grown just before arriving in Washington was now scraggly. Lincoln's appetite lessened, and he had lost almost thirty-five pounds from his already-lean frame. Only Mary could coax him to eat, and he would obey her without protest, but when she was absent he frequently forgot about meals. Because he was so anxious, he no longer slept in the master bedroom of the White House. When he didn't stretch out on a cot in his dressing room, he would spend the night at the telegraph office across the street, waiting for news dispatches from the battlefront.

The hope for an early Union victory in the war between the states had long since evaporated. Without military force to back up his order to free the slaves in the South, slavery continued, despite the Emancipation Proclamation.

Because of poor leadership and management, the Union army was not able to consistently defeat its Confederate foes. Confronting Secretary of War Cameron with his failures and shady dealings, Lincoln asked him to resign and replaced him with Edwin Stanton, a tough, religious administrator. Stanton's enemies called him ruthless, and there are many who believed that the only man Stanton ever respected was Abraham Lincoln.

One of President Lincoln's most difficult decisions of the war was whether or not to permit exchanges of prisoners of war, so that the prison camps might be emptied and the captive soldiers could rejoin their respective armies. Lincoln decided, amid much criticism, to refuse an exchange. He reasoned that the Union army could always be replenished with immigrants pouring into the North from Europe. The Confederates had only the men raised on Southern soil. If those soldiers taken prisoner by the Union could be prevented from rejoining the Confederate army, the South would have to surrender that much sooner. In addition, Union prisoners would need to be fed and guarded by Confederate soldiers, who would have to be taken away from the battle lines.

Conditions, particularly for the Confederate army and the Union prisoners, were appalling. Thousands of Union soldiers died in the poorly supplied prison camps. The Confederates were short of provisions, and they fed their Northern prisoners the same food that their own soldiers ate. The pork fat, dried peas, and corn were inadequate, and disease among the soldiers was rampant. The Union soldiers, enraged at what they perceived to be deliberate torture and murder of Northern prisoners by the Confederates, toughened the conditions in their own prison camps, and Southern prisoners began to die in huge numbers.

Lincoln knew that his refusal to exchange prisoners meant the deaths of thousands of men, both Union and Confederate. Yet he believed that choosing that course would end the war sooner. He felt it was the right thing to do, no matter what the consequences were.

Lincoln's confidence in his generals increased as the war progressed. General Grant didn't seem to care how many men he lost as long as he won battles — and win he did, over and over again. General Sheridan was driving his troops through the South, while General Sherman earned an awesome reputation for shedding Confederate blood and destroying Confederate cities.

Despite his worries about the war, Lincoln still did his best to administer his other presidential duties. At his desk by early morning, he worked through the day, constantly interrupted by well-wishers and office seekers who lined the corridors of the White House. Lincoln tried not to refuse an audience to anyone, but visitors cut into his time. He frequently had to work past midnight, when the office was quiet, to finish the day's business.

Since young Willie Lincoln's death, his brother Tad had been utterly spoiled by his parents. Though the boy loathed schoolwork, he was tenderhearted and as honest as his father. Lincoln always made time for his son in the evening hours, listening to an account of his boy's day and answering his many questions. Often Lincoln's last duty at night was to carry little Tad, sound asleep, to his small bed upstairs.

Tranquil moments such as these, however, did not last long in the White House. Ward Hill Lamon, a federal marshal, was constantly worried about President Lincoln's safety. Twice since the beginning of the war, a sniper had fired at Lincoln on the dark road as he rode his horse alone at night. Lincoln brushed off Lamon's concern. He declared that the bullets were probably fired by hunters, though each shot tore through his clothing, nearly wounding him.

Everyone begged Lincoln to be more cautious. Secretary Stanton ordered round-the-clock guards, whom Lincoln often evaded when he wanted to be alone. Lincoln was not being deliberately stubborn, but feelings of Providence made him believe that if his life were the price for the restoration of the Union, then so be it. In any case, he did not think he would live long after the war ended.

Lincoln's dreams during the war years were strange and disturbing. He had an odd vision of his own face in a double mirror. One face was the image he was accustomed to seeing, while the other was a death-like mask. Mary, a great believer in dreams, interpreted this to mean that her husband would be re-elected to a second term as president, but would not live through the second term. Lincoln also had a recurring dream about sitting in a boat coming swiftly toward the shore. This dream occurred with uncanny precision right before several of the Union's greatest victories. Lincoln came to believe it was a symbol of hope and a sign that the war was drawing to a close.

When General Hooker's Union Army of the Potomac met the Confederate Army of Northern Virginia in Chancellorsville on May 1, 1863, General Lee's forces smashed the Union troops. Hooker was demoralized, and his army was shattered. Without hesitation, Lincoln named General George Meade to take over.

General Meade, uncertain and startled by his sudden promotion, heard that General Lee's troops were pushing into Union territory in Pennsylvania for the first time. The Confederates were desperately seeking fresh ammunition and supplies. The two opposing armies finally met in a historic battle near a little town called Gettysburg on July 1, 1863.

The Battle of Gettysburg was the engagement that turned the tide of the war in favor of the North for good. For three blood-drenched days, 90,000 Northern troops battled 75,000 Southern troops. Soldiers fell by the thousands on each side. But when the fighting ended, the Union forces emerged victorious in one of the most important battles of the Civil War. Though Union casualties were over 17,000 men, Confederate General Lee counted over 20,000 casualties and saw his army destroyed. As a result of this vital loss of manpower, the Southern army would never mount a major offensive again.

General Meade could have chased the retreating Southern troops and perhaps captured the whole force, thereby shortening the war greatly. But he did not follow them, content to rest his exhausted troops in shelters from the pouring rain. Once more the Confederates escaped more casualties and surrender.

President Lincoln, Secretary of War Stanton, and several other government officials maintained a tense vigil at the telegraph office across from the White House throughout the battle. As word came through the wires of retreats and attacks, they alternately rejoiced or slumped in despair. During those three terrible days, Lincoln spent every waking minute in the tiny office, staring at the telegraph keys and willing them to deliver the news he desperately wanted to hear. He could not be persuaded to leave the office for meals or rest. No other single action of the war cut such harsh worry lines into his face.

Throughout the Battle of Gettysburg, Mary continued her own tradition of visiting the Soldiers' Home in Washington to pay her respects to wounded Union soldiers who were brought there to recover. When the war began she had started bringing them small gifts of fruit and flowers, hoping to bolster their spirits, and she was warmed by the kindness with which she was always greeted.

One day, as the Battle of Gettysburg raged on, Mary was in the presidential carriage on her way to the Soldiers' Home. Suddenly she was thrown to the side of the carriage as it lurched forward. Annoyed, she peered out of the carriage to scold her coachman, but he had mysteriously disappeared. Mary turned white with terror as she realized the driver had been thrown from his seat and the terrified horses had bolted out of control. She sat quaking with fear as the carriage raced furiously along, rocking precariously from side to side, until at last it crashed into the side of a sturdy tree. Mary was taken to the hospital, unconscious. She had suffered a minor concussion.

An investigation disclosed that someone had slipped into the stables and loosened the driver's seat just enough so that he would be thrown off at the first turn. It was obviously another attempt to assassinate President Lincoln.

Mary had recovered completely from her accident by the time the Gettysburg battlefield was commemorated in a special ceremony on November 19, 1863. Unfortunately, young Tad Lincoln was now ill, and she refused to leave him to journey to Pennsylvania. Lincoln traveled by train to Gettysburg with several members of his cabinet.

Originally, the organizers of the ceremony had not intended to ask Lincoln to speak. They had engaged Edward Everett, the famous Massachusetts orator, to address the crowd, and no one really believed that Lincoln could say anything worthwhile after Everett's oration. But someone finally extended an invitation to him to make a short address to the crowd, and Lincoln, though aware that the invitation was late, accepted promptly.

Some sources claim that on the train to Gettysburg, Lincoln scribbled a few sentences on the backs of discarded envelopes, trying to organize his thoughts before he faced the crowd. Historians now generally agree that this is not true. They say that he actually took great care in preparing what he was going to say.

Edward Everett was the main attraction on that warm, sunny November morning. His stirring address covered the better part of two hours, and the crowd cheered when he finished. At last Lincoln was introduced, and he rose, holding a single, long sheet onto which he had copied his speech.

Abraham Lincoln, the sixteenth president of the United States, faced the crowd. His dark, brooding eyes sadly surveyed the audience as he began to speak in his usual high-pitched voice. Lincoln's text took a mere five minutes to deliver, and the applause was only polite when he sat down. Lincoln whispered sadly to Stanton that apparently his audience was not impressed. He was right. The newspapers covering the ceremony spoke in glowing terms of Everett's speech, but few recognized the splendor of Lincoln's Gettysburg Address.

Abraham Lincoln's noble words, though largely overlooked at the time, have inspired many generations of Americans. Most historians believe that Lincoln wrote five careful drafts of the Gettysburg Address, and not one of them was hastily scratched on the back of a brown envelope. No matter how Lincoln created his speech, his words still ring with conviction and sincerity.

"Four score and seven years ago our fathers brought forth upon this continent a new nation, conceived in Liberty, and dedicated to the proposition that all men are created equal.

Now we are engaged in a great civil war, testing whether that nation, or any nation so conceived and so dedicated, can long endure. We are met on a great battlefield of that war. We have come to dedicate a portion of that field, as a final resting place for those who here gave their lives that that nation might live. It is altogether fitting and proper that we should do this.

But, in a larger sense, we cannot dedicate — we cannot consecrate — we cannot hallow — this ground. The brave men, living and dead, who have struggled here, have consecrated it, far above our poor power to add or detract. The world will little note, nor long remember, what we say here, but it can never forget what they did here. It is for us the living, rather, to be dedicated here to the unfinished work which they who fought here have thus far so nobly advanced. It is rather for us to be here dedicated to the great task remaining before us — that from these honored dead we take increased devotion to that cause for which they gave the last full measure of devotion — that we here highly resolve that these dead shall not have died in vain — that this nation, under God, shall have a new birth of freedom — and that government of the people, by the people, for the people, shall not perish from the earth."

10

Ending the Civil War

HAD THE TIDE of war not begun to swing toward a Union victory, Abraham Lincoln probably would not have been re-elected president in 1864. By the time he returned to Washington after his Gettysburg Address in November of 1863, he could do little to help his re-election effort, because almost immediately he fell ill with what doctors diagnosed as a mild form of smallpox. As Lincoln lay in bed, he wondered humorously where all the favor seekers were now.

Lincoln's advisers also believed his chances of re-election were slim. The end of the war was no nearer in mid-1864 than it had been two years previous, and Lincoln's administration did not appear to have brought the nation closer together. Many poor men bitterly resented the draft policy that would permit a man to stay out of the army if he could pay $300 to another man to take his place. The Northern radicals believed Lincoln was not taking a ruthless enough approach to the South while the Northern liberals believed he was being too harsh.

Many men were competing for the Republican nomination, including Salmon Chase, the secretary of the treasury, and Secretary of State William Seward. They knew that the next president would almost certainly be called on to supervise the reconstruction of the nation. They felt that Lincoln had already shown far too much sympathy toward the Confederacy, and that the South would get off far too lightly in the upcoming years. As expected, the Democrats ran General McClellan as their candidate for president and pledged to voters that they would stop the war immediately and restore the Union.

To make matters worse, Lincoln had received a letter from Jefferson Davis, a former Mississippi senator who was now the president of the Confederacy. The letter stated that the only Northern peace proposal that Davis would accept would be one based on the recognition of the Confederacy as a separate nation.

Then two major events turned the uncertain election into an inevitable and sizable victory for Lincoln. His generals were winning battle after battle in the South, and the news was reassuring the population that President Lincoln was in firm control of the country.

First came the incredible news that General Grant had routed Confederate troops in Vicksburg, Mississippi after placing the entire city under siege. Union forces now occupied the fallen city and controlled the entire Mississippi River. It was a major victory that assured a speedy end to the war. Then there was General

Sherman's remarkable march through the Deep South to the city of Atlanta, Georgia. After a fierce battle on September 2, 1864, Sherman telegraphed to Washington that "Atlanta is ours, and fairly won . . ." It was not expected that the presidential candidate would pick the person who would run as vice-president, for in those days that was the party's task. Instead of choosing incumbent Vice-President Hannibal Hamlin as Lincoln's running mate in the 1864 election, the Republicans made a startling new choice for their vice-presidential nominee. They chose Tennessee governor Andrew Johnson, a staunch Union supporter.

Lincoln helped his re-election by ordering home the Union troops so that they might vote in their hometowns. The Northern armies had been very loyal to the president, and he knew that their votes could swing the election in his favor. Lincoln was right once again. The Lincoln-Johnson ticket resulted in an overwhelming victory for the Republicans. Lincoln now believed that he would see not only the war's end, but the compassionate rebuilding of the Union.

Inauguration day on March 4, 1865 found President Lincoln calm and quiet, while Vice-President-elect Andrew Johnson was terrified. Outgoing vice-president Hannibal Hamlin helped to calm Johnson as a huge crowd gathered at the Capitol Building to witness the swearing-in ceremony. Lincoln stepped forward to take the oath of office for the second time and give his inaugural address. The man who recited the oath, however, did not look like the same person who had spoken the same words only four years earlier.

Lincoln's rapidly graying head was bowed, and his shoulders slumped as he faced the crowd. His famous homespun humor was visible only in flashes. His entire frame showed the pressure of four years of agonizing war. As Lincoln peered at his one-page inaugural address, a young man in the crowd strained forward, a pistol concealed in his hand. The young man was John Wilkes Booth.

Lincoln spoke gently of his wish to return the South to its lawful place in the nation. He affirmed that it could only be accomplished with kindness, and "with malice toward none, with charity for all." He pleaded, "to bind up the nation's wounds; to care for him who shall have borne the battle, and for his widow, and his orphan — to do all which may achieve and cherish a just and lasting peace."

As the president finished his short speech and sounds of applause thundered around the podium, Booth carefully aimed at Lincoln and pulled the trigger. Incredibly, there was no blast from the pistol. Booth looked down, bewildered as President Lincoln disappeared from view. Booth had neglected to release the safety catch on the gun.

At the time of his second inauguration, Lincoln's home life was in a state of disarray. Mary Lincoln had received a number of polite but subtly threatening notices from merchants to whom she owed money. She was vastly relieved that her husband had won a second term in office, because now her creditors would not bother her for the next four years.

In addition, during the war, many of Mary's Kentucky relatives had enlisted in the Confederate army, a fact that greatly distressed her. No household more clearly demonstrated the split between brothers and blood relatives caused by the war than the Lincolns. Though Mary considered herself a Union patriot, her family was staunchly Confederate, and many refused to see her. To make matters worse, three of her brothers were killed in the first few years of war, leaving several of her sisters-in-law nearly penniless. Lincoln gently offered them aid if they would sign the oath of loyalty he required of all captured Confederates. They proudly refused. Mary saw her own family, the Todds, slipping away from her.

Robert Lincoln was also causing trouble. He had begged his father to allow him to enlist in the army, but Lincoln refused. Mary had already lost two sons; he doubted she could live through the death of a third. As the years passed and young Robert remained a civilian, newspapers and rival politicians pointed to him as a blot on his father's record. How could he be permitted to remain safe when so many thousands of other young men were fighting and dying?

Robert's repeated pleas to his father to allow him to fight finally brought results. Worn down by his son's persistence, Lincoln finally agreed and looked for a relatively safe position in the army for his boy. Robert was given a captain's commission and became an aide to General Grant.

At the beginning of Lincoln's second term, there were other problems that needed to be addressed as well. The new currency or "greenback" was slipping in value, while the price of gold was skyrocketing. Lincoln worried about the economic stability of the coun-

In a rare tranquil moment in 1864, President Lincoln pauses from his official duties to spend time reading with his son Tad

try. America was in debt for almost half a billion dollars, and where would the money come from for rebuilding the nation after the war ended?

There was also the question of what to do with the newly freed Southern slaves after the war was over. Lincoln understood the insecurity of the Southern whites, who were accustomed to giving orders to blacks, not treating them as equals. How could blacks blend into a prejudiced Southern society, even though they were guaranteed the freedom to do so? Of course, ending the war was still the biggest problem Lincoln faced.

The South was finally crippled after four long years of war, their armies destroyed. Most of their proudest cities had been forced to surrender after long sieges. There was almost no ammunition or food left in the Confederacy. Her brightest and best young men were dead or wounded, her rich land plundered and stripped, beautiful homes burned to the ground. Penniless refugees wandered in search of food and shelter.

Yet in Washington, peace delegations from the South continued to ask for recognition of the Confederacy as a separate country. Lincoln always refused. His terms to end the war were simple — the South must return to the Union without slavery. Nothing else would be accepted. The delegations could not find a way to compromise. There was no room for negotiation in his terms.

Despite the devastation of their cities, land, homes, and manpower, the South proudly rejected Lincoln's terms. Though fighting on meant certain destruction and continued starvation, the Confederacy refused to give in to return to the Union. That being so, Lincoln knew that peace would come only when one of the two armies had fallen to its knees.

Reluctantly, Confederate General Lee sent word to Union General Grant that he would meet him to discuss terms of unconditional surrender. The opposing generals chose a farmhouse in the small settlement of Appomattox Courthouse, Virginia as their meeting place. The Union and Confederate forces arrived there on the morning of April 9, 1865. It was Palm Sunday, the Sunday before Easter.

Many hours later, Secretary of War Stanton received word from General Grant of the Confederate army's impending surrender. Stanton hurried to the White House to tell President Lincoln what had occurred that morning in the Virginia sunshine.

The ragged remains of the Union and Confederate armies faced each other warily. Among the weary Northern soldiers was Robert Lincoln, who proudly wore his captain's uniform. He had seen much fighting, but had not participated in it.

Meanwhile, Grant and Lee met inside the courthouse. The Confederate general wore his best gray uniform, his long, shiny sword clanking smartly at his side. Beside Lee's erect and dignified figure, Grant appeared dumpy and somewhat shabby. His long blue coat was open and his vest was buttoned haphazardly. The contrast between the two men was startling, and each seemed costumed for the other's role. Lee held himself proudly, like a conqueror. Grant, in his disheveled appearance, strongly resembled the humbled enemy. Yet Grant greeted Lee with genuine warmth, explaining politely that he had not had time to polish his own sword for the ceremony.

Both men had attended West Point Military Academy and served in the American army during the Mexican War, and they respected each other's abilities under combat pressure. Now he represented that native state and the ten others that made up the Confederacy in defeat.

Grant seemed relaxed and began to lead the silver-haired Lee into a casual discussion about the Mexican War. Lee soon joined comfortably in the conversation and, in a few minutes, he began to relax his stiff courtesy.

Finally, though, Lee changed the subject by saying that they had best discuss the business at hand. Both armies were, after all, waiting outside. Grant nodded reluctantly and seated himself at the table in the center of the room.

Swiftly, he wrote out a simple document of surrender, listing the concessions he expected of the South. The Confederate soldiers were to leave their armies and go home. They would not be disturbed by the United States government if they kept their word not to fight again. Enlisted men would turn in their weapons, though officers would be permitted to keep theirs.

General Lee nodded as he read over the terms. They were generous. As he laid the document down on the table he made a request. Would General Grant allow the members of the Confederate army to keep their horses? Lee explained that many of the animals would be used in spring plowing. They would be sorely missed if confiscated, and the enlisted men were too poor to buy new ones.

Grant agreed that the men could keep their horses, and added that those without horses would be permitted to take one each from the Union army's store for their journey homeward.

Lee read over the revised terms with satisfaction. "This will have the best possible effect on the men," he said at length. "It will be very gratifying and will do much toward conciliating our people." He reached for the quill pen in its inkstand and signed his name carefully on the bottom of the page. Grant added his own signature.

Then Lee remarked, with gentle pride, that his men had had nothing to eat in recent days besides parched corn. Grant snapped an order to his aides. Any Union soldier who had three rations was to hand over two of them. Quartermasters were ordered to open the Union commissaries. The Southern soldiers would be provided for before they turned slowly homeward. Lee thanked him again, and the two generals departed in opposite directions.

As the Southern general approached his starving, ragged troops, the men crowded around him, crying. Tears poured down Lee's face as he told them quietly, "I have done the best I could for you." He looked over the Confederate troops. Of the 49,000 men he had begun with, less than 27,000 remained. The rest lay in crude graves or had deserted long ago to try to scratch out a living on their plundered farms. Lee bowed his head at the ragged scarecrows of men he saw on all sides.

Grant's steel-hard face was equally unhappy as he sat with his staff after the surrender. After firing off a telegram to Washington affirming that the war was indeed over, he sat wearily all afternoon, telling old yarns about his Mexican War days. No comment about the painful event of the morning crossed his lips, not once.

On April 9, 1865 Secretary of War Stanton told Lincoln the most welcome news of his presidency — the Civil War was finally over. The next morning's newspapers related the terms of surrender and assured the Union's citizens that the war between the North and the South was over.

The people reacted with hysterical joy. Monday became a day of wild celebration. Stanton ordered five hundred military guns to blast a tribute to peace, a tribute whose thundering roar broke many windows on Lafayette Square. Government offices and many businesses were closed. The relieved population, hearing that Lincoln had returned to the capital, congregated at the White House, eager to hear their president speak to them.

President Lincoln tried to spend his morning concentrating on state business, as usual, but the thunderous noise outside made quiet work impossible. Even young Tad added to the waves of cheers and celebration. He seized a captured Rebel flag, stationed himself in front of one of the White House windows, and waved it energetically.

Finally Lincoln appeared. He told the shouting, cheering throng below that he would make a formal speech the next night, but the masses of men, women, and children wanted something now.

Something they could remember.

Lincoln waited patiently for the yells and shouts to die away. When they did not, he asked the White House band to strike up the Southern anthem "Dixie." "I have always thought 'Dixie' was one of the best tunes I have ever heard," he told his audience. "The rebels had taken it as theirs, but the Union has recaptured it — and so it is our lawful prize." The cheers rose in a mighty crescendo. Lincoln quietly slipped inside. Lincoln knew that reuniting the North and South would take more than signing a peace agreement or playing 'Dixie.' The task of reconstructing the Union would be as long and difficult as the war just completed. There were many important considerations, and Lincoln had to weigh them all in order to plan the next few years.

From the beginning, he had insisted on kindness and charity toward the conquered states of the South. Nothing could be gained by humiliating them, or by punishing them. He knew they had lost enough. Over half a million Southern soldiers lay in graves scattered from Gettysburg to Georgia. The plantations were stripped bare. The homes were plundered. The slaves were suddenly free. The Southern way of life had to change, and Lincoln wanted to make that change as gentle as possible.

Millions of dollars would be needed to fund the struggling farmers and help them rebuild their lives. In March, Congress had already approved the formation of the Freedmen's Bureau, an organization to help freed slaves find homes and jobs. Although they were free, most blacks would continue their lives on the land where they had been slaves. They would need education and help in adjusting to their new status. Lincoln knew the former slave owners would be bitter at the idea of competing with their former slaves in farming.

If some of the blacks were also permitted to vote, the bitterness could become violence. The former slaves and former slave owners were going to have to live side by side.

In the last year of the war, Lincoln had slept fitfully, his nocturnal hours often broken by nightmares and visions. With the coming of peace, however, his dreams turned prophetic. Soon after the surrender, President Lincoln, his wife Mary, and several friends sat together in the White House. The talk turned to dreams and visions, and Lincoln mentioned that he had had a disturbing dream some time before. The others pressed him to tell it, and at last he began: "About ten days ago, I retired very late. I had been waiting up for important dispatches. I could not have been long in bed when I fell into a slumber, for I was weary. I soon began to dream. There seemed to be a deathlike stillness about me. Then I heard subdued sobs, as if a number of people were weeping. I thought I left my bed and wandered downstairs.

"There the silence was broken by the same pitiful sobbing, but the mourners were invisible. I went from room to room. No living person was in sight, but the same mournful sounds of distress met me as I passed along. It was light in all the rooms: every object was familiar to me, but where were all the people who were grieving as though their hearts would break?

"I was puzzled and alarmed. What could be the meaning of all this? Determined to find the cause of a state of things so mysterious and so shocking, I kept on until I arrived in the East Room, which I entered. There I met with a sickening surprise.

"Before me was a catafalque [raised structure], on which rested a corpse in funeral vestments. Around it were stationed soldiers who were acting as guards; and there was a throng of people, some gazing mournfully upon the corpse, whose face was covered, others weeping pitifully.

" 'Who is dead in the White House?' I demanded of one of the soldiers.

" 'The President,' was his answer. 'He was killed by an assassin!' "

Mary Lincoln was horrified by the dream, and his friends urged Lincoln to be more cautious. There had been much talk in the government about the possibility of a presidential assassination. As a result, Secretary of War Stanton arranged for a bodyguard of four policemen to guard President Lincoln at all times. He especially warned Lincoln to stay out of public places, to limit appearances in theaters and on the roads. However, despite the precautions made, there was nonetheless a feeling of jubilation with the war just ended. Most people did not believe that an assassination could happen, but President Lincoln had watched four years of war and suffering, and now peace had come — but probably not without a price.

11

Assassination at Ford's Theatre

THE MORNING OF April 14, 1865 began cheerfully. Despite the gray sky and drizzle outside, the Lincolns gathered for a lighthearted breakfast. It was particularly festive because Capt. Robert Lincoln had recently returned from the battlefront. The family, such as it remained after the deaths of Eddie and Willie, was complete and together again.

Mary announced that she had tickets to Grover's Theatre for that evening, and though they were staging a lavish celebration, she would prefer to see the actress Laura Keene in her last night of *Our American Cousin* at Ford's Theatre. The president assured his wife that he would find a way to get some tickets to the performance. Mary offered the Grover's tickets to Robert. He accepted them.

The president spent a good part of the morning in his office, receiving visitors who desired his help in minor matters. During a short pause, he sent a messenger to James R. Ford, the manager of Ford's Theatre, requesting the State Box for himself, Mrs.

Lincoln, and General and Mrs. Grant. The theater owner, Mr. Ford, was delighted. Publicized attendance by the president would guarantee a full house, and during Easter week, traditionally the worst theater week of the year, theaters were seldom full. Ford immediately ordered bunting to be laid around the box, and a special comfortable rocker brought into the box for the president's use.

General Grant could not attend the performance that evening. He told the president, with some embarrassment, that he and his wife were going home to New Jersey to see their children. The general hadn't seen his family in a long time, and now that the war was over he was eager to make the trip. Lincoln understood and excused him.

The president asked his secretary to find another couple to replace the Grants. That turned out to be a difficult assignment. No other general stood in such favor with the president and Mrs. Lincoln. Secretary of War Edwin Stanton curtly refused the invitation. He never attended the theater, and he believed the president should not, either. Personal violence against government officials was a very real threat. Several other cabinet members were out of town. Lincoln's private secretary had to be cautious about extending invitations to just anyone, because Mrs. Lincoln often quarreled with political friends of her husband. At the last minute, the secretary secured an acceptance from Miss Clara Harris, daughter of the senator from New York. Her fiancé, Major Henry Rathbone, would accompany her. They were not exactly political celebrities, but they were the best choice possible.

In the afternoon, Mary Lincoln asked her husband to take a ride with her in a private carriage, saying he looked pale and could use some fresh air. Lincoln agreed, and as they drove along his face became more and more cheerful. It was after five o'clock, and the daylight was fading. Mary plainly saw the merry twinkle in his eye and the smile stretching across his face.

"You almost startle me by your great cheerfulness," she remarked.

He agreed that he was cheerful. "I never felt so happy in my life."

Mary's smile faded. "Don't say that," she murmured.

"Why not, Mother? It is true." Lincoln often called his wife by the pet name "Mother."

Mary's eyes filled with fear. "Because the last time you said those same words was just before Eddie died."

Abraham and Mary Lincoln returned to the White House in silence.

Our American Cousin was a light comedy, not the type of play Lincoln would have chosen to attend. He preferred Shakespeare. As the Lincoln party entered the Presidential Box at Ford's Theatre, the play stopped and the audience rose to cheer their commander-in-chief. President Lincoln smiled and acknowledged the ovation. Then he sat down in the rocker, and the play went on.

Some time after the first act, John Parker, the president's bodyguard, left the door to the State Box unattended and went downstairs to the bar for a drink. It was Parker's responsibility to keep all intruders away from the president, but he was often irresponsible and took his duties lightly. That very evening he had reported almost an hour late for service. Because he left his post without a word to anyone, he left a clear path for anyone who wanted to reach the president.

One man did. He was John Wilkes Booth, a twenty-five-year-old actor from the well-known family of actors. John Wilkes had spent most of his life over-shadowed by the memory of his father and the continuing triumphs of his brother Edwin, then considered America's greatest Shakespearean actor.

John Wilkes acted frequently in theaters across the country, but he was an unprofessional, shallow young man who was always forgetting his lines and cues. His best performances were supplemented by all manner of athletics. He often leaped from balcony to stage, fired prop guns, and bellowed his speeches in a loud, ring-ing voice — when he could remember them. He had matinee-idol features. His thick, curling black hair, ivory skin, elegant moustache, and huge liquid eyes melted ladies' hearts wherever he played.

Tonight, however, he was acting not in a play, but in a deadly real drama. Before morning, if all went well, he would easily overshadow the fame of his father and brother. As a Southern patriot, John Wilkes Booth believed it was his duty to assassinate the president and destroy the Union government.

Originally Booth's plan had been to kidnap the presi-dent and demand the freedom of all Confederate prisoners in exchange for his release. As Booth, along with a small band of conspirators, ran into one delay after another, the end of the war approached. Finally, Booth decided that the only way to save the Confederacy would be to kill Lincoln and other key members of the government.

One of the conspirators was assigned to murder Secretary of State Seward in his sickbed, another to kill Vice-President Johnson. Booth himself drew the assignment of shooting President Lincoln.

As the third act of the play began, Booth quietly entered the Presidential Box, a derringer in his hand. Lincoln, Mary, and their guests were so engrossed in the play that no one noticed him. Mary asked Abraham if he thought the audience would mind if they held hands. He said, "They won't think anything of it." These were the last words Lincoln spoke.

A roar of laughter exploded from the audience in response to the funny dialogue. Booth raised his derringer and fired at point-blank range at the back of the president's head. Lincoln slumped forward in his chair. He did not utter a sound.

Mrs. Lincoln and the others turned curiously at the sound of the gunshot. They saw a young man, pale with excitement, holding a smoking gun, and Lincoln slumped over, apparently unconscious. To them, Booth said simply and quietly in Latin, "*Sic semper tyrannis!*" (Thus always with tyrants!) Booth pushed himself toward the edge of the box, and Major Rathbone, without quite realizing what had happened, lunged at him.

Booth dropped his pistol and drew out a large hunting knife. He slashed at Rathbone, slicing his arm through his coat all the way to the bone. As Rathbone

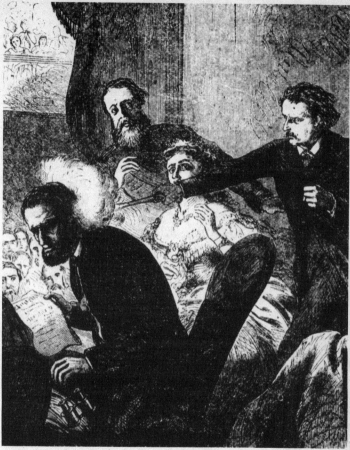

John Wilkes Booth shot President Abraham Lincoln during
a play at Ford's Theatre on April 14, 1865. Lincoln died the next
day. The United States government offered a $100,000
reward for the capture of the "murderers of our beloved
president"

staggered, Booth cried to the people below, "Revenge for the South!"

On stage, Harry Hawk, the actor playing one of the leading roles, realized something was terribly wrong. He and the bewildered audience looked up at the box in time to see Booth poise himself on the edge of the box and hurtle down toward the stage.

Even in his last appearance, John Wilkes Booth bungled his exit. He had failed to take into account the bunting that hung on the edge of the box and caught his spur in the heavy silk. When he fell to the stage, a bone in his left ankle snapped.

Nonetheless, Booth staggered off the stage, into the wings, and past the horrified acting company, to the stage door. There a stagehand named Edward Spangler had a fast horse waiting, and despite the broken ankle, Booth threw himself into the saddle and galloped madly into the nearby state of Maryland. As he rode, he hoped the other conspirators had succeeded in assassinating Vice-President Johnson and Secretary of State Seward. If these three officials were dead, the Union would be left leaderless. Fortunately, both Johnson and Seward survived the attacks on their lives.

Panic followed in the theater. The first doctor to offer his services was twenty-three-year-old Charles Leale, an assistant surgeon of the United States Volunteers. He thought at first that the president had been stabbed, because Rathbone, now bleeding profusely, was so obviously the victim of a knife attack. But when Leale lifted the president's head and saw the bloody hole, he knew that Lincoln had been shot. It was immediately apparent that the bullet had not emerged. It was lodged in the president's brain.

Other doctors hurriedly appeared, but Leale remained in charge. He knew the president was dying, and he insisted that they move him from the theater at once. It was suggested that he be taken back to the White House, but Leale refused, saying he would never survive the trip. He directed them instead to a house across the street.

The nearest house, at the edge of F Street and Tenth, stood dark. At 453 Tenth Street, the house next door, the owner beckoned to them. His name was William Petersen, and he was a tailor. Hastily the soldiers carried Lincoln into a small, spare bedroom and laid him down gently on the bed. The death vigil began.

Secretary of War Edwin Stanton, urgently summoned to the president's side, arrived and took charge of the chaos unfolding before him. Mary Lincoln, alternately screaming and crying, was ordered out of his sight. Robert Lincoln, dazed and horrified, wept through the night.

The doctors knew they had no antidote for Lincoln's fatal injury. They tried to keep his body warm, but nothing could restore his consciousness. As the sky turned light the next morning, Lincoln began to moan. The eye, behind which the fatal bullet had lodged, turned black. The doctors brought in Mary Lincoln. She stared, grief stricken, at the scene in front of her — her oldest son sobbing and her husband's life fading. In a moment, they led her out again.

Finally, at 7:22 A.M. on April 15, 1865, Lincoln took his last breath. The room was utterly still.

Stanton looked at the dead president and said quietly, "Now he belongs to the ages."

Abraham Lincoln, the sixteenth president of the United States, was dead from an assassin's bullet. The Union he had fought so hard to preserve would now be under someone else's protection and guidance.

Lincoln's body lay in state, first in the East Room of the White House, just as he had dreamed, then in the rotunda at the Capitol Building. Thousands of people wearing black came to pay their respects, to weep over the dead president's body, and to express their shock. Flags were lowered to half-mast, a sign of respect for the dead leader.

The army took charge of funeral rites for the dead president. The ceremony in Washington was solemn. Union troops marched, bearing a flag. Behind them walked a riderless single horse, with boots reversed in the stirrups, the symbol of a dead hero. Across the nation, millions of people grieved for their lost president.

Finally, Lincoln's body was put on a special train to Springfield, Illinois, where he would be buried. En route, the train stopped in various cities and towns so people could gather around it and pray. Never before had a president been murdered in office. The grief and outrage for the crime poured out of Americans from state to state. On May 4, 1865, twenty days after he was shot, Abraham Lincoln was buried in Oak Ridge Cemetery in Springfield, Illinois.

12

Justice for the Assassins

JOHN WILKES BOOTH'S plot to destroy the Union government failed, even though he succeeded in assassinating President Lincoln. One of Booth's co-conspirators, Lewis Paine, failed, though just barely, in his attempt to kill Secretary of State Seward. George Atzerodt, a third co-conspirator, could not even bring himself to attempt to kill Vice-President Johnson, who, upon Lincoln's death, was sworn in as the seventeenth president of the United States.

After making his way from Ford's Theatre, John Wilkes Booth talked his way past the sentry at the Navy Yard Bridge and escaped into Maryland. He hid on the dark road until he caught sight of a fourth co-conspirator, David Herold, who was riding for his life. The two went on together, stopping to pick up guns at a pre-arranged hideout. They rode sixty miles through the dark night, but Booth's injured ankle was causing him blinding pain. He had to stop to have it tended.

The only doctor Booth knew in the area was Samuel Mudd, a slave owner and Southern sympathizer, so Booth and Herold headed to Mudd's home. The doctor agreed to treat the injured man. Booth had covered his face with a false beard and a dark neckerchief. He splinted the ankle with the supplies at hand and put the patient to bed.

The two fugitives rested through the next day, although Mrs. Mudd's suspicions were aroused by their odd behavior. For one thing, Herold had requested a straight razor so that his injured companion might shave. Yet when Mrs. Mudd looked at Booth later the beard was still there. It appeared to her that the beard was false. News of the murder of President Lincoln was only beginning to filter into the countryside, because the telegraph wires from Washington had been mysteriously cut just after Booth fired the shot.

Booth and Herold requested the use of a carriage so that they might continue their journey resting comfortably. Mudd reported that no carriage was to be found. It was Easter Sunday, and most of the farmers wanted to keep their carriages for their own use. Booth and Herold would have to leave on horseback, as they had come. Late that afternoon, the two mysterious men mounted and rode away.

Dr. Mudd was sufficiently suspicious to tell the military personnel in town. They questioned him about the man's injury and how he had treated it, and asked for descriptions of the two men. Mudd knew Booth, who, he recalled, had bought a horse in the county the previous winter. Mudd insisted he didn't recognize the injured man as Booth.

Booth and Herold hid in Zekiah Swamp, a stretch of undergrowth and quicksand occupied only by a few black freedmen. They asked a black man to show them the way to the Cox farm, where they knew they could count on Southern sympathy and help.

The man obliged, and Booth and Herold faced Colonel Samuel Cox at his home. They asked for help, and he called on his foster brother, Thomas A. Jones, who owned a farm close by.

Jones was reluctant to help, even though he had risked his life continually during the war, ferrying Confederate visitors to the Potomac. But his reservations disappeared when he met Booth, now deadly pale from the pain in his ankle and still heroically handsome. It seemed that Booth's theatrical appearance could inspire sympathy in almost anyone. Jones promised to bring them food every day and take them across the river when it was safe to do so.

Meanwhile, a massive manhunt was immediately launched from Washington. Agent Lafayette Baker, head of the Northern secret service, took his orders directly from Secretary of War Stanton. The government sent out posters offering huge rewards for the capture of the conspirators — John Wilkes Booth, David Herold, and John Surratt. Surratt's mother Mary ran a boardinghouse in Washington. From the beginning of the investigation, the military had targeted the boardinghouse as the meeting place of the conspirators. Mary Surratt was placed under arrest immediately, while troops scattered south to search out Booth's hiding place.

The government had some good luck at the Surratt boardinghouse. As they were waiting for Mrs. Surratt to gather some personal items to take with her, a man with a pick over his arm knocked at the door. It was Lewis Paine, Secretary of State William Seward's attacker, who claimed to be a laborer hired to dig a gutter for Mrs. Surratt. But he could not answer the question of why he had appeared so late at night. The nearsighted Mrs. Surratt, who had only met Paine dressed as a minister, was not wearing her spectacles. Seeing him in rough clothes, she denied ever having known him. The officers arrested him immediately.

Once in custody, Paine refused to admit that he had attacked Seward, but a servant at the Seward residence easily identified him. Paine was clapped into prison and shackled with leg and wrist irons. A heavy cotton bag was placed over his head and was kept there twenty-four hours a day. Eventually, all the conspirators arrested would be shackled in similar fashion and forced to wear the same suffocating bags over their heads.

Meanwhile, Booth and Herold were spending an uncomfortable week in the swamp. They nervously waited for farmer Jones to judge the climate safe enough for them to escape. When Jones heard that the Union cavalry thought they had spotted the fugitives in another village, he told Booth and Herold to get ready. While the military was off on a wild-goose chase they could secretly slip away by night.

At last Jones brought the fugitives to the Potomac River, helped them into a flat-bottomed, twelve-foot boat, handed Herold the oars, and pointed the way. He mentioned that a Mrs. Quesenberry would help them if they told her Thomas Jones had sent them. Once more, the assassins set off.

The strong tides in the Potomac River defeated Booth and Herold so they had to wait until the next night to row to safety. They managed to get to Mrs. Quesenberry, and were sent on to a Dr. Stuart. They hid for a while in Gambo Creek just north of Dr. Stuart's home, but something frightened them there. They fled, leaving behind Booth's coat, his diary, empty brandy bottles, a wallet containing $2,100 in Union money, and letters of credit on Canadian and British banks. An Indian tracker recovered the items and returned them to Washington. The fugitive's trail was growing hotter.

Booth and Herold reached Port Conway, Maryland and crossed the river to Port Royal, Virginia. Once there, they needed shelter. An ex-Confederate named Willie Jett suggested that the Garretts, who had a farm in nearby Bowling Green, would take them in.

The unsuspecting Garretts warmly welcomed Booth and Herold. They agreed to let Booth stay, while Herold went into town to buy new shoes. The next day the Garretts were surprised to see both Herold and Booth bolt toward the farm's tobacco barn when Southern riders passing by called out that Northern troops were nearby.

Their guests' behavior aroused the Garretts' suspicions. Jack, the oldest son, believed they were probably horse thieves. Although he agreed to let them spend the night in the barn, he followed them, locked them in, and gathered the older boys around him. They weren't going to steal the Garretts' horses, not if Jack and the others had to sleep in the corncrib nearby to watch them!

Based on a tip, with the 16th New York Cavalry, Agent Baker arrived at the Garrett farm at four in the morning on April 26, eleven days after Lincoln's death. They woke the household, demanding to know where the fugitives were. Terrified, Garrett said that they were sleeping in the tobacco barn; his sons were nearby to keep an eye on them in case they tried to steal any horses.

Agent Baker shoved young Jack Garrett toward the barn, telling him to instruct Booth and Herold to lay down their arms. Jack was frightened, knowing that the fugitives were armed. The cavalry plainly heard Booth shouting at Jack to get out before he shot him. Baker called to Booth to surrender. Booth refused, but added that Herold wanted to surrender. Herold came out of the barn, hands raised, and was arrested immediately.

Agent Baker ordered the cavalry to pile brush and hay around the barn. He was going to set it afire and smoke out the assassin within. As the flames began to blaze, a single shot rang out. Booth fell forward, and the soldiers rushed in to snatch him out.

Sgt. Boston Corbett had fired at Booth through the cracks in the barn door. When his enraged superior officer asked him why, he answered, "God Almighty directed me."

"Well," the officer answered, "I guess he did, or you couldn't have hit him through that crack in the barn."

Lt. Colonel Everett Conger was dispatched to Washington to announce that Booth had been found and was dying. Twenty minutes after Conger spurred his horse toward the capital, Booth lay dead.

Meanwhile, the new president Andrew Johnson ordered the arrests and trial of the conspirators as the most important piece of government business. The police arrested anyone they thought might have had any possible connection to the murder. This included Edwin Booth, John Wilkes Booth's brother, who had never agreed with his brother's political views; John Ford, the owner of Ford's Theatre; and the entire cast of *Our American Cousin*. Ford's Theatre was ordered closed at once, and was eventually confiscated by the government to be made into a government administration building.

John Wilkes Booth's death excited much emotion, and Lafayette Baker was concerned that angry crowds would try to harm the body. Accordingly, he accompanied the body aboard the ironclad ship, the *Montauk*. After an identification commission had confirmed that the body was indeed that of John Wilkes Booth, Baker and several others put the coffin into a small rowboat. It was late at night as the crowd on board the ship watched the small boat glide into a marshy area of the Potomac River used as a burial ground for condemned government horses.

Once the rowers were sure that the crowd could no longer see them, they slipped quietly away to the nearby Arsenal Penitentiary. A grave had already been dug beneath a stone slab in one of the lower convict's cells. There they dumped Booth's body and carefully covered it. No one was to know where Booth was buried. Some years later, however, his remains were removed, sent home to the Booth family, and reburied in the family plot.

After Lincoln was buried, President Johnson and Edwin Stanton concentrated on what came to be called the Conspiracy Trial of 1865. The trial began the second week in May, not quite a month after Lincoln's assassination.

There were nine defendants: Lewis Paine (attempted to murder Secretary of State Seward), Mrs. Mary Surratt (conspirator), George Atzerodt (assigned to kill Vice-President Johnson), David Herold (aided Booth's escape to Virginia), Dr. Mudd (set Booth's broken ankle), John Surratt (conspirator), Ned Spangler (stagehand who had held Booth's horse at Ford's Theatre), Michael O'Laughlin (assigned to kill U.S. Grant), and Samuel Arnold (conspirator). They were tried not in civil court but by military tribunal, an unusual procedure for civilians. All were accused of treason and murder.

The trial lasted until June 28. Two days later the verdict was delivered. Eight of the defendants were found guilty as charged. One defendant, John Surratt, was not convicted. Paine, Atzerodt, Herold, and Mrs. Surratt were sentenced to die by hanging. Spangler, the stagehand, received six years at hard labor in prison. Conspirators Arnold, O'Laughlin, and Dr. Mudd were sentenced to life imprisonment at hard labor.

Mrs. Surratt's death sentence was met with outrage. Never had a woman been hanged in the entire history of American justice.

On the afternoon of July 7, 1865, the four convicted felons were hanged in a public ceremony in Washington. The other four were sent to the military prison at Dry Tortugas, Florida.

Conditions in the prison were appalling, with disease raging throughout. Michael O'Laughlin died in prison, and President Johnson pardoned Ned Spangler, Samuel Arnold, and Mudd in 1869.

13

The Aftermath of Lincoln's Death

AFTER PRESIDENT LINCOLN'S death on April 15, 1865, Andrew Johnson became the seventeenth president of the United States and took over Lincoln's program of Reconstruction, or the rebuilding of the South. Though his original views toward the South were harsh, President Johnson came to believe that Lincoln's sympathetic approach toward the defeated South was correct. Johnson began to adopt Lincoln's policies whenever possible, causing resentment among several unsympathetic radical Republican cabinet members. Even so, Johnson had asked all of Lincoln's cabinet members to remain in office.

The rebuilding of the South that Lincoln had hoped to achieve peacefully and with kindness became violent, disorderly, and very bitter. Secretary of War Edwin Stanton imposed harsh restrictions on the former Confederacy. Northern troops were quartered in every major city. They watched the ragged Southern population at every step. No man who had owned property before the war or fought in the Confederate army could vote. The singing of the Confederate songs such as "Dixie" or "Bonnie Blue Flag" became a crime. Instead of the help Lincoln had wanted to provide the South, the harsh radical Republicans offered suspicion, fear, and misery.

The Republicans despised Johnson's approach to Reconstruction and brought pressure on Congress to impeach and remove him from office. In 1869, President Johnson was brought before Congress. A two-thirds vote was necessary to impeach the new president. Andrew Johnson was saved from dismissal by a single vote. Secretary Stanton, leader of the radical Republicans, was the force behind the impeachment, but when Congress failed to impeach President Johnson on May 26, 1868, Secretary Stanton was crushed and resigned his cabinet post.

Meanwhile in the South, the Freedmen's Bureau failed in its goals to bring widespread education and financial relief for the former slaves. Waves of violent crimes committed by both blacks and whites swept the devastated Confederacy.

The Ku Klux Klan, a group made up of former Confederates, sprang up almost as soon as the slaves were freed. Klan members secretly met at night, dressed in pointed white hoods and capes, and sought to punish blacks, whether they were innocent or guilty of a crime. Because former slaves were threatened, horsewhipped, or even hanged, Northern troops swore to hunt down and hang every Ku Klux Klan member they could find.

Had President Lincoln lived to carry out his program of "malice toward none, charity toward all," it is likely that much of the pain in the South could have been prevented. Ironically, Lincoln's death at the hand of a Confederate assassin was a great loss for the South.

The loss to those who knew Abraham Lincoln was even greater. His wife Mary never recovered from the assassination. She was so hysterical that she was unable to attend her husband's funeral. Years of migraine headaches and the tragedy of her children's deaths had shaken her terribly. With the death of her husband and her son Tad, who died six years later in 1871, all stability remaining deserted her. Her oldest and only remaining son Robert regretfully committed her to an insane asylum. She was released four months later and went to live in Europe, but her hallucinations and fears of being murdered continued until her death in 1882.

Tad's death left Robert Lincoln the only surviving child of the former first family. He was married and had a young daughter. Later, he became secretary of war, and witnessed the assassinations of Presidents James Garfield in 1881, and William McKinley in 1901.

Billy Herndon, Lincoln's last law partner, was deeply grieved over his friend's death. Herndon turned his efforts to memorializing Lincoln, and became his first official biographer. To the end of his life, Herndon sought to present a true, unflinching portrait of the man he had known in Springfield.

Major Henry Rathbone and Clara Harris, who had accompanied the Lincolns to Ford's Theatre on the fatal night, were married and set up a household in Germany. In 1883, the major tried to kill his children in a fit of lunacy. A nurse intervened, and instead, Rathbone shot his wife and then stabbed himself. Doctors saved him, but he spent the rest of his life in a German insane asylum.

John Parker, the bodyguard who had left his post and therefore left a clear path for Lincoln's assassin John Wilkes Booth at Ford's Theatre, was never punished. He continued in the security force until 1868, when he was found sleeping in a streetcar while on duty. After his dismissal, he disappeared.

Sgt. Boston Corbett, who had shot Booth in the Garrett barn, became a celebrity of sorts and eventually was given a job as doorman for the ladies' gallery in the Kansas state legislature. One morning he entered with two revolvers and inexplicably fired on the legislators and the ladies in the gallery. He was subdued and committed to an insane asylum in Topeka, Kansas, but escaped.

Edwin Booth, John Wilkes Booth's brother, was released from prison and continued his distinguished acting career, and died in July 1893. On July 9, his coffin was carried to the New York church where services would be held. During that same hour in Washington, the upper floors of Ford's Theatre collapsed, killing twenty-two people and injuring sixty-eight others. Some of the medical records stored there, including those of the inquest on John Wilkes Booth's body, were destroyed by fire. Ford's Theatre was eventually restored and is now a museum of Lincoln memorabilia.

EPILOGUE

Lincoln's Legacy

THE DRAMATIC AND tragic death of Abraham Lincoln did not overshadow the achievements of his life. His great, lasting contribution was to restore the North and the South into a united nation once again. Beyond that, he tried to correct flaws in the Constitution by declaring the Emancipation Proclamation. By the time Lincoln died, he had done his best to see that people of all races living in the United States would be entitled to life, liberty, and the pursuit of happiness.

Perseverance and opportunity are synonymous with Abraham Lincoln. Despite the hard circumstances of his birth, he struggled and worked to improve himself beyond the accepted status of his family. His life was a continuous climb upward and striving for achievements. Yet the qualities that brought him to the presidency remained with him all his life. He prized industry, intelligence, and especially honesty.

No matter what he did, those qualities always formed the foundation of his character.

Lincoln is admired and respected as one of the greatest presidents of United States. In a time of torment, he opposed popular opinion to make changes so that all Americans could be free. That decision took untold courage and faith that he could follow the right path for his country. His childhood on the frontier and the many books he had read about the heroes of the Revolutionary War who had fought and died to establish a country of peace and liberty profoundly influenced Abraham. Lincoln believed in the fight the Founding Fathers had waged, and he could not allow their struggle to die in the argument over slavery and states' rights. Like George Washington, Thomas Jefferson, and Benjamin Franklin, Lincoln's greatest priority and deepest concern were that "government of the people, by the people, for the people, shall not perish from the earth."

It was an agonizing path, but it was the right path. From his boyhood, all the way to the highest office in the land, Abraham Lincoln, the Freedom President, always chose the right path for himself and his country.

APPENDIX

Unanswered Questions

MANY QUESTIONS STILL remain concerning the conspiracy surrounding Abraham Lincoln's assassination. The only question answered without argument is the question of who pulled the trigger at Ford's Theatre. Everyone agrees that it was John Wilkes Booth.

However, what happened after Booth left the theater raises doubts and arguments among historians. Many disagree with the conclusions set forth by the government in the Conspiracy Trial. Here are just a few of these unanswered questions and their possible answers.

Was the murder plot planned by the confederate government?

Some historians argue that John Wilkes Booth was acting under orders from high officials in the con-

116

federate government. Among those officials were Jefferson Davis, president of the Confederacy, and Judah Benjamin, his secretary of state. They may have believed that the murder of Lincoln would disrupt the Union government enough to buy them some time to reassemble their weakened and failing Southern armies.

This theory is supported by the fact that Booth considered himself a Southerner, though he never enlisted in the Confederate army. As a prominent celebrity whose face and name were known all over the country, Booth had access to the highest officials in the Southern government and would have considered it an honor to strike a blow for the Confederacy in her dying hour.

In addition, there is well-documented evidence that Booth's original plan was to kidnap President Lincoln and then exchange him for all Confederate prisoners held in the North. If successful, this plan could have strengthened the Confederate army with much-needed manpower. Certainly it would have been attractive to the Confederate leaders.

The theory is probably not true, however, because both Jefferson Davis and Judah Benjamin were in full flight by the last chaotic days of the Civil War. Penniless and alone, they were in no position to supervise a plot to kidnap or to kill Lincoln. In addition, both Davis and Alexander Stephens, the Confederacy's vice-president, had served with Lincoln in Congress. They knew Lincoln to be an honest, fair, and compassionate man. Whatever their political differences with him, they probably realized that their best hope for the future of a defeated South lay in Lincoln's mercy.

Was Lincoln murdered by Northern radical Republicans?

The most popular theory in recent years is that Lincoln's death was engineered by the radical Republicans, the group of Northerners belonging to the Republican party who wanted to see the South punished. Many radical Republicans held high posts in Lincoln's cabinet, and his desire to gently reunite the Union after the war ran contrary to their desire for revenge.

This theory suggests that every step of the government investigation of the assassination was part of a gigantic cover-up. Secretary of War Edwin Stanton, who could have masterminded the plot, was the director of the murder investigation. Some suggest that he may have destroyed or falsified important evidence.

When Booth escaped from Washington after shooting Lincoln, high-level Republican officials, such as Stanton panicked. They arrested everyone with the slightest connection to the crime and began to manufacture evidence they could use in an upcoming trial. They could announce that they had killed Booth, which would direct public attention to the trial of the conspirators in Washington. This theory says that Stanton fully intended to rig the trial and rid himself of the conspirators, thus erasing the last links that could trace the conspiracy back to him.

118

Also implicated in the plot are prominent Northern businessmen, bankers, and United States senators. Supposedly Booth was introduced to them all. However, Booth saw that these men cared nothing about the South, except for the money they could make from it. As a result, he decided to act independently of them. But he did have documents that would implicate these men to the murder plot. The most revealing document was his diary, which contained the names of all the men with whom he had conspired as well as the amount of bribe money many of them received.

Was John Wilkes Booth really killed?

There is considerable speculation that John Wilkes Booth never set foot in Bowling Green after the assassination; that another man, a look-alike, was cornered there and shot; that the body was falsely identified as Booth and buried, even though the government knew they had the wrong man.

While looking for Booth, the cavalry also intended to find another suspect, Capt. James William Boyd, a Confederate who had been imprisoned in Washington and now worked for the War Department.

Boyd bore a strong physical resemblance to Booth. At forty, he was much older than Booth, but he wore a sweeping moustache, his build was the same, and his initials JWB, like Booth's, were inked on the back of his hand, just as Booth's were. Some historians say that after an elaborate switch, it was Boyd — not

Booth — who was cornered in the Garrett barn in Bowling Green and shot by Boston Corbett.

Was John Wilkes Booth's body properly identified?

This theory says that the identification commission on the *Montauk* was rigged from the beginning. The only people permitted to see the body either did not know Booth very well or had not seen him for some time. They were not told that Booth had shaved his moustache at Dr. Mudd's house, which would not account for the full moustache on the corpse. Only Dr. John Franklin May, who had treated Booth for a neck growth some time before, was troubled about the remains. He said the face looked much older, and he didn't remember the actor as having freckles. Booth, in fact, had an ivory complexion without a single blemish, while Captain Boyd, his look-alike, had reddish hair and freckles. Yet after Dr. May's statement had been taken — and some revisions made in ink by an unknown hand — the doctor wrote a private statement saying that he had never seen such a change in a man's face in such a short time. In addition, though Boyd did have a leg wound like Booth's, his was on the right leg. History tells that Dr. Mudd had treated Booth for a broken bone in the left ankle.

What became of the real John Wilkes Booth?

If John Wilkes Booth did not die in the Garrett barn, what happened to him? Some historians speculate that Booth eventually escaped to Harpers Ferry, where he stayed for a short time on a farm with his ex-wife Izola Darcy. Around November of 1865, Booth supposedly reached Pennsylvania, went on to New York City, and then fled to Canada. It is said that eventually Booth sailed to England, where he married Elizabeth Marshall Burnley, a woman he had known prior to the assassination of Lincoln. Some time later, the theory goes, he traveled to India, where he supposedly died.

There are other reports that Booth moved to California, united with his first wife, and had a son by her. A man who died in Enid, Oklahoma in 1900 claimed on his deathbed to be John Wilkes Booth. If Booth did, in fact, go to India and fake his death, he could have returned to the United States and lived out his life under another name. The body of the Oklahoma man was mummified and still exists. Many believe this is the real body of John Wilkes Booth.

Did the conspirators receive a fair trial?

There are some historians who believe that the trial of Lincoln's assassins was a farce. The government wanted the case closed to their satisfaction, and therefore they did not strain themselves to provide attorneys for the accused. The conspirators were expected to find their own counsel, and when they did, often the lawyers were defending more than one person at a time. The lawyers were not permitted to meet with their clients before the trial began, and could only converse with them in open court as the proceedings went on.

Were government witnesses bribed or threatened?

Some historians theorize that to guarantee the conviction of that all nine conspirators, the government brought in several witnesses, all of whom had been paid and coached extensively on their testimony. Others, such as Louis Weichmann, a boarder at Mrs. Surratt's establishment, were threatened with arrest if they did not give testimony favorable to the prosecution. Later, when Mrs. Surratt was hanged, Weichmann said sadly that he believed she was innocent. Yet, his testimony was key in convicting her.

Will the whole truth about Lincoln's assassination ever be known?

Despite the scenario told in history books and popularly repeated, many questions remain about the murder of Abraham Lincoln. Since everyone involved is now dead, piecing together the facts may prove impossible. If so, it is a mystery that will endure. Once John Wilkes Booth disappeared with his secrets on that dark April night in 1865, no one can state positively what really happened to him or what true facts lay behind the murder of Abraham Lincoln.